THE
CHURCH IN BRISTOL

A Short History

by

RUPERT E. DAVIES

(Tutor in Church History at Didsbury College, Bristol)

with illustrations by Reginald Dymond

D1437602

Published by
JOHN WRIGHT & SONS LTD.
BRISTOL
1960

To STEPHEN AND JUDITH

Printed in Great Britain by John Wright & Sons Ltd.,
at the Stonebridge Press, Bristol

PREFACE

THIS book is chiefly for the schools of Bristol, and is designed to fit in with Bristol's *Agreed Syllabus of Christian Education*. But I very much hope that it will be of help to all who wish to trace the working of the Holy Spirit in the life of a great city throughout its history.

It is written, as will soon be plain to all readers, from the conviction that there is one, and only one, Church of Christ, to which all the denominations (a word which I detest, but am forced to use) which worship Jesus Christ as God and Saviour belong. Those who do not share this conviction will not, however, I think, be prevented from gaining from the book the knowledge they would like to have.

Any writer of Church History is in a difficulty when he comes to write the words 'Church' and 'Churches'. I have written 'church' and 'churches' to mean a building or buildings. I have written 'Church' to mean both the one Church of Jesus Christ and each of the denominations into which it is at present divided, and 'Churches' to bear the latter meaning—since I can find no other way of dealing with the situation.

RUPERT E. DAVIES
April, 1960.

Didsbury College,
Bristol.

CONTENTS

CHAPTER 1

The Dark Centuries

MANY FACTORS have combined to make Bristol what it is today—climate, geography, the configuration of the land, the fluctuations of trade and industry, the changes in the political structure of England, the temperament which results from the mixture of West Country blood with that of South Wales and farther afield, and many other things. But nothing has played a larger part than the Christian Faith. No one who lives in Bristol is unaffected by the city's religious past; there have been times in Bristol when religion was the most important concern of all, more important even than the overseas trade which has guaranteed the city's prosperity through the centuries.

Nobody knows how it all began. But then, nobody knows exactly how Bristol itself began. In pre-Roman times there was a rocky ford across the Avon, just under the present Suspension Bridge, with some fortified camps on the heights above to defend it from marauders. The Romans did not build a town where Bristol stands today, but some of the wealthier settlers had farms or villas in the neighbourhood, and at Sea Mills there was a port for shipping from across the Severn, for soldiers and travellers who wished to come from the walled town of Caerwent (*Venta Silurum*) to the waters at Bath (*Aquae Sulis*).

How many Christians lived in these parts during the Roman occupation there is no means of telling. We know, of course, that Christianity first came to Britain with the Roman soldiers; for we cannot place much credit in the Glastonbury tales about Joseph of Arimathea. There are traces of Christian worship and belief from Roman times in various parts of the country—the remains of chapels in

Lullingstone, Kent, and Silchester, Berkshire, the *Chi-Rho* sign (the first two letters of the Greek word for Christ) on the mosaic pavements of Roman villas, the 'palindrome' found near Cirencester.* Three bishops from Roman Britain, from York, London and Caerleon, attended the great Church Council of Arles in Gaul in 314, not long after the first British martyr, Alban, had been executed for hiding a Christian priest from the soldiers of the Emperor. Forty-five years later some British bishops attended another Church Council, at Ariminum, in North Italy, and were so poor that some of them accepted the Emperor's offer to pay their expenses, though this was thought to be a great humiliation. But none of this has any known connexion with Bristol. There were, no doubt, some Christians here, and that is all that we can say.

When the Roman legions were withdrawn from this country in A.D. 407 to defend Italy against the barbarian invaders, the political structure of Britain fell into ruin, and the culture which the Romans had laboriously planted withered and died. The Christian Church shared in the general decay. In fact, the only real sign of life was the vigour with which the battle about Christian teaching was carried on between the followers of Pelagius and St. Augustine of Hippo. Pelagius was a Briton, perhaps from the West Country (but he was called 'that great fat dog of Britain, stuffed with Scottish porridge' by his enemies), who maintained a view, still widely held by Englishmen, that we can get into the Kingdom of God by our own efforts; St. Augustine said that we are much too weak-willed and corrupt to do anything of the sort, and

* This is the so-called 'Corinium acrostic' and runs like this:

```
R O T A S
O P E R A
T E N E T
A R E P O
S A T O R
```

This could be translated 'Arepo the sower holds the wheels with an effort'. It can be read from right to left as well as from left to right, and from bottom to top as well as from top to bottom. It contains all the letters of 'Pater Noster', the first two words of the Lord's Prayer in Latin, and is probably a secret Christian sign from the days when the Christians were persecuted.

that only the grace of God can bring about our salvation. The Church as a whole declared St. Augustine to be in the right, but Pelagius maintained his view with great vigour in many places. He did not spend much time in his own country, but his followers here carried on the struggle on his behalf, and a certain Germanus had to be sent from Gaul to counteract their teaching.

Probably the Angles and the Saxons, who were emphatically not Christians, when they drove the Britons into the West, drove the Christians among them in the same direction. At any rate the next burst of Christian activity took its origin on the West coast, perhaps on the shores of the Bristol Channel. Here the great St. Patrick, son of a deacon and grandson of a priest, grew up, only to be kidnapped by pirates and taken to Ireland at the age of sixteen. He escaped by boat to Gaul, where he formed the resolve to go back to Ireland and preach the Gospel. In 432 his resolve was carried out, and with astonishing courage and power he planted the Christian Church on the land and in the hearts of the Irish people. From Ireland St. Columba, a man of fiery zeal and courage in the tradition of St. Patrick, but recently shamed by his part in the slaughter of three thousand men in civil strife, set out for Scotland and landed on the island of Iona. Here he founded a monastery and a model agricultural community, and from here his missionaries set out for many parts of Scotland, and, in 633, for the kingdom of Northumbria at the invitation of its king, Oswald.

So there were Christians in many parts of the British Isles when Pope St. Gregory the Great sent St. Augustine, one of his own monks from the city of Rome, to convert the angel-like Angles in 597. There were Christians of Celtic race in Wales and Cornwall, and perhaps farther East; there were many Christians and a strong Christian Church in Ireland; in Scotland the Church was expanding rapidly and was about to extend its activities to England. St. Gregory may not have known much about all this, and St. Augustine on his way through Gaul was so terrified by tales of the unmitigated ferocity of the pagan English that he returned to Rome. But the Pope sent him back to his task, and he must have been greatly relieved to find that the king of Kent had a Christian wife, the daughter of a Frankish king.

St. Augustine's mission was immediately successful, but within a rather limited area of South-Eastern England. An attempt to evangelize the North by the work of Paulinus, who became the first Archbishop of York, broke down after a few years' success, and the real evangelists of Northern England were the missionaries from Iona, especially St. Aidan. The Pope had given St. Augustine authority over all the Christians in England, presumably including the Celtic bishops in Wales and the West. This was a tactless move to make without first becoming aware of the true situation. The Celtic bishops took umbrage, and a conference between them and St. Augustine was arranged. There is a local tradition in Bristol that this conference took place on what is now College Green, in front of the site of the Cathedral. But Bristol was not important enough for this to have really happened, and it is more likely that the scene was near Aust, to which the bishops from Wales could make an easy voyage. But no place can take much pride in the conference, for it broke down in disagreement, and was even, according to some authorities, followed by actual fighting between the followers of St. Augustine and those of the Celtic bishops. Certainly the rift was not healed.

For the years round about the middle of the seventh century the Celtic bishops from the West made common cause with the Celtic Christians centred in Lindisfarne (the monastery founded by St. Aidan off the coast of Northumbria) against the alleged interference of the missionaries based on Canterbury. The argument in theory was about the right way to date Easter, to cut monks' hair and to administer the Sacrament of Baptism, but the truth is that the two kinds of Christian had different conceptions of Christianity, which they did not take the trouble to try to reconcile for the sake of the vast task of evangelism which lay before them. It was an unholy strife.

The Synod of Whitby met to settle the matter in 664.

King Oswy of Northumbria adjudged the issue in favour of the monks from Canterbury, and so took the step which made the Church in England an integral part of the Church which stretched across Europe under the authority of the Pope. The Celtic Christians in England were left without royal support, and had to submit or leave for Ireland; the Church throughout the country was gradually brought into line—not without some resistance—with Roman customs and beliefs.

Bristol, as we have seen, played little or no part in these events which settled the direction of English Christianity for many centuries to come. But it seems to have been growing steadily as a cluster of houses near the junction of the Frome and the Avon, under the name of Bricgstowe, 'the place of the bridge', and before the Norman Conquest it was large enough to have a mint of its own. The earliest Bristol churches were certainly built in Anglo-Saxon times and probably well before the Conquest. There are many rivals for the position of 'the first church in Bristol'. The issue can be left to be fought out between a number of churches near Bristol Bridge —All Saints', Holy Trinity (now Christ Church), St. Maryleport, St. Peter's, St. Ewin's and St. Werburgh's (of the two last, the former has ceased to exist, the latter has been moved from the centre of the city).

But from the point of view of the Church at large Westbury-on-Trym was more important than Bristol up to 950. There was a monastery of the Benedictine Order there before the year 800, and it suffered much from the Danish invasions of the ninth century which ravaged England far and wide. At the beginning of the tenth century there was a reform of Benedictine monasteries throughout England, led by St. Dunstan, Abbot of Glastonbury and later Archbishop of Canterbury. He was determined that the monks should really keep their vows of poverty, chastity and obedience, and at his instance St. Oswald, Bishop of Worcester, made the monastery of Westbury, which lay in his diocese, a model for other monasteries to follow.

The repeated Danish invasions and the consequent political instability had reduced both Church and State in England to a low level of effectiveness by the time that William I extorted by force the fulfilment of Edward the Confessor's promise that he should be the next king of England. Thus William had a good excuse for doing what he would no doubt have done in any case. He placed Normans whom he could trust in nearly every position of authority and importance in the realm and in the Church. But he left one bishop in his see who had been there before 1066, and that was St. Wulfstan, Bishop of Worcester, whose character and competence no one could criticise.

Bristol, like Westbury-on-Trym, was just within St. Wulfstan's diocese, and things were happening there which the Bishop could not tolerate. Some of the Norsemen had settled on the coast of Ireland, and wanted servants to wait upon them. Apparently they thought that English boys and girls were more reliable, or better-looking, than Irish ones, and sent traders to Bristol to buy them as slaves. The business flourished, until St. Wulfstan came down from Worcester, not once but many times, and denounced it, at least temporarily, out of existence. St. Wulfstan was the first of a long line of Bristol Churchmen to condemn a social evil in the name of the Christian Faith.

CHAPTER 2

The Church in a
Medieval Town

IT WAS AFTER THE NORMAN CONQUEST that the civic
life of Bristol really began. William I saw the military importance of the town's position, and probably the first Bristol
Castle was built during his reign. Robert of Gloucester, son
of Henry I, turned it into a redoubtable stronghold, to curb
any thoughts of rebellion against the king in the minds of
the feudal lords of the West; it contained a mighty rectangular
keep of stone which lasted till the days of Cromwell.

This Robert did between 1120 and 1130, and when he had
thus served the king he proceeded to serve God by founding
the Priory of St. James (now represented by the Church of
St. James Barton). The Priory was subordinate to the Abbey
of Tewkesbury, and followed the Benedictine Rule, like the
monastery at Westbury-on-Trym. This meant that the
monks prayed in the chapel in winter at 2 a.m. and six
more times at intervals through the day and the evening, and
went to bed at 8 p.m. In the summer they went to bed
and rose for prayer a little later. The Rule of Benedict laid
down that when the signal was given they should 'rise without delay and rival one another in their haste to the service
of God'; and went on: 'and when they rise for the service of
God, let them gently encourage one another, because the
sleepy ones are apt to make excuses'. But they were to work
as well as pray—for, said the Rule, 'idleness is the enemy of
the soul'. There was heavy manual labour to be done, and
much study of books. Many monks were set to the copying
out of manuscripts, others to the teaching of those who came

for instruction, and others to the nursing of the sick in the monastery's hospital, which was open not only to the monks, but to all who were brought there for healing. No brother possessed any property of his own, not even the most trivial; he was provided with all that he was expected to need by the head of his monastery, and he was not thought to need very much—just a cowl, a tunic, shoes, stockings, a girdle, a knife, a pen, a needle, a handkerchief and writing tablets. No letters or gifts could be received, except by permission of the Abbot or the Prior.

The reign of Stephen (1135–54) was marked by civil war of the most savage kind, and Stephen himself spent part of it as a prisoner in Bristol Castle. But the town, protected by its castle, was left in comparative peace, and its commerce seems to have grown steadily. Then in 1140 Robert Fitzharding founded an Augustinian Abbey, which later became the Cathedral, on grassy slopes outside the town. Fitzharding was *prepositus* of the neighbourhood, a royal official appointed to collect customs duties and exercise general supervision; he was not a great feudal baron, but a member of a powerful local family which had acquired wealth and land by trade and royal favour. He did not very lavishly endow the Abbey which he founded, but its Chapter House is superbly planned and built. The monks of the Abbey were Canons who followed the Rule ascribed to St. Augustine of Hippo, slightly laxer and more general than that of Benedict, and encouraging the brothers to engage in parochial work outside the walls of their monastery.

By a judicious mixture of military strength, successful trade, and adherence to the winning side in most civil conflicts, Bristol's size and importance grew steadily during the century which followed. True to the spirit of the times, the great men of Bristol founded several 'hospitals' for the old and the sick to live in. One for leprous women was set up between Bedminster and Redcliffe. The most famous and enduring was St. Mark's, founded jointly in about 1220 by Maurice Berkeley de Gaunt, a grandson of Robert Fitzharding, and Robert de Gournay. It was called 'The Gaunts', and so has given its name to a building used for different purposes today, while its chapel is now the Lord Mayor's Chapel. A Master and three priests looked after a hundred poor people, only some of whom lived actually in the hospital, and taught them trades and 'mechanic arts'.

We have come to a time when a new religious movement was sweeping over Europe. It arose from the vision and the work of two men, very different in temperament and character, but very similar in purpose, St. Francis and St. Dominic. Francis (1181–1226) was a rich merchant's son who literally 'sold all that he had and gave to the poor' at the direct command, as he believed, of Jesus Christ. From then on he lived with his friends a life of the utmost gaiety and simplicity, begging his food, and wandering from place to place to preach the love of God and banish the dread of evil spirits which infested the minds of everyone in Europe except the highly educated. He even went to Palestine to convert the Saracens and so stop the Crusades. Such a life as his was bound to kindle the imagination and rouse the enthusiasm of thousands of young men who wished to take their religion seriously, and the Franciscan Friars with their grey habits and their simple pictorial preaching were soon to be found in all the countries of Europe.

Dominic was a grim and austere Spaniard who called out the complete loyalty of his followers by his utter devotion to duty and truth. His Order was first founded to teach Christian truth to those who had fallen into error in Southern France. It soon extended its teaching ministry over the cities and universities of Europe, and the Dominican Friars in their black and white habits were as well known as the Franciscans.

The Franciscan Order was at first vowed to complete poverty, not only for the individual members but for the Order as a whole. Not a building, not a book, was its own. But the Dominican Order was allowed to own books, as an aid to teaching, and it soon became the most learned body of men in Europe. Somewhat later the Franciscan Order changed its Rule to allow the possession of books, and became as learned as its sister Order, which was also sometimes its rival.

By 1300 each of the two Orders had more than fifty houses in England. The Dominicans arrived first in Bristol, and settled down east of St. James in 1227. The Franciscans followed soon after, and found a home in Lewin's Mead in 1234. Both Orders were notable not only for their piety, preaching and learning, but also for their exceptionally clean conduits of running water.

The College of Westbury (as the monastery there was called) had had many ups and downs since its foundation in the eighth century; sometimes it was lost to the Benedictine Order altogether, and was inhabited by members of other Orders. George Giffard, Bishop of Worcester from 1268 to 1302, decided to make it more important than it had ever been before. He did not get on very well with the monks of his own Cathedral Chapter at Worcester, and preferred living in his palace in Henbury. He ordained many clergy in Henbury and Westbury, and wanted Westbury to be another

Cathedral Chapter with the same rights and authority as the Chapter in Worcester. The Worcester monks did not take to the idea, and long and bitter controversy broke out, which had to be settled by the Pope after Giffard's death. The ruling went against Westbury, which remained a College consisting of a Dean and five prebendary monks.

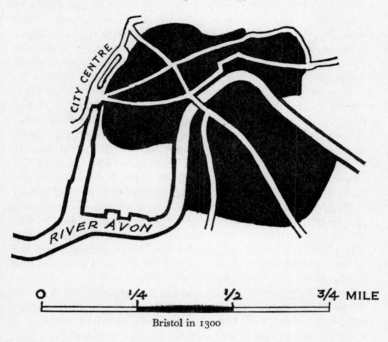

Bristol in 1300

Between 1250 and 1320 the burghers of Bristol were not so successful as they had been in the past in taking the right side in political struggles. They revolted against Edward II, and were put down and punished. Then Edward II himself was brought to ruin, and the town suffered again for being a stronghold of Edward's adherents. The general effect of Bristol's participation in the civil wars of this savage period was that it lost much of its political importance for the rulers

2

of the nation, and was able to resume its commercial progress without much interference.

St. Augustine's Abbey suffered much from the troubles of the times and the preoccupation of its possible benefactors with political affairs. But Edmund Knowle, who became Abbot in 1306, was a man of determination and enterprise. He persuaded the Bishop of Worcester to put some funds at his disposal, and enlisted once again the financial help of the Berkeleys, the descendants of Fitzharding and the traditional patrons of the Abbey. Among other things he re-built the Choir and the Lady Chapel, and transformed the whole appearance of the Abbey Church.

In spite of the Black Death and the Hundred Years War, which wrought havoc in every part of English life, and not least in the Church and its monasteries, the merchants of Bristol exported wool and manufactured cloth in growing quantities and built up the town's commercial greatness. It was during this period of great difficulty for much of the country that the great church of St. Mary Redcliffe received most of its present glories. Redcliffe was at first a suburb of Bristol, outside the town and rivalling its parent in prosperity, but later it was included in Bristol, somewhat against its will. There was a church there from the early twelfth century, but now, between 1320 and 1380, the main structure of the church as we know it arose. It was built in Late Decorated and Early Perpendicular style, by the design and work of many men of vision whose names are hard to discover. It is sometimes unkindly suggested that the splendours of St. Mary Redcliffe were partly due to the desire to rival the Abbey Church across the river, and we cannot definitely say that such a motive was absent from the minds of the builders, for there was still some tension betwen Bristol and Redcliffe; but St. Mary Redcliffe was always a Parish Church, while St. Augustine's was then an Abbey, devoted to monastic purposes; so there was no real opportunity for competition, and no evidence of any has survived.

We know from many sources that the spiritual life of the Church in England was not in a very healthy state at the end of the fourteenth century. The great age of medieval piety and sacred learning was over; the Pope, the spiritual head of Christendom, instead of watching over the Christian world with fatherly care from Rome, was living in luxury as the captive of the French king in Avignon; the more powerful clergy in England seized as many offices and livings as they could lay their hands upon and drew the income from them all, while others were 'possessioners', owning large estates and revenues to which they gave far more of their attention than to the welfare of their flocks. Besides, many Englishmen were out of sympathy with the Church because they could not see why large taxes should be sent to the Pope in France, with which country England was more or less permanently at war.

The spokesman of the widespread social and religious discontent was John Wycliffe (1329–1384). Wycliffe was not an altogether attractive man. He was Master of Balliol College, Oxford, very learned, and not very skilful in communicating his profound ideas to others less learned than himself. He was a man of fierce temper, who was further embittered by opposition. He was guilty, in a mild way, of one of the vices which he condemned in other clerics, that of holding more than one ecclesiastical office. But he put into vehement speech and action what many of his countrymen felt deeply, and he has been called by his admirers the 'Morning Star of the Reformation', since he anticipated many ideas which the Reformation brought to the notice of the Church.

At first, under the protection of John of Gaunt, the most powerful politician of the time, he issued his protests without hindrance and gained much support. But when he attacked the teaching of the Church of the time about the Holy Communion, and denied that the bread and wine were changed into the Body and Blood of Christ, John of Gaunt ceased to support him, and he was forced into private life, and retired to be the Rector of Lutterworth in Leicestershire. His teaching was officially condemned, and forty-four years after his death his body was exhumed and burned, and the ashes thrown into a stream. But his influence lived on through the

Bible in English which he had been helped by Nicholas of Hereford and John Purvey to produce, and through the activities of the Lollards, simple priests who had imbibed his ideas, and went about preaching them out of reach of the authorities for many decades after his death.

Wycliffe's link with Bristol was that he was Prebendary of Aust in the College of Westbury-on-Trym. He was personally instituted to the office, but it is not certain that he ever visited the neighbourhood again, though he still held the prebend when he died. It is probable, however, that his disciple, John Purvey, worked in Bristol, and it may well be there that he put the finishing touches to his English translation of the Bible (the second to be inspired by Wycliffe), which was published in 1388. We do not know for certain that there were Lollard preachers in Bristol, for their movements were kept very secret, but the readiness of Bristolians in later generations to hear teaching which conflicted with that of the official Church suggests that they probably had an attentive audience if there were.

But the events connected with Wycliffe brought no serious disturbance to the religious life of Bristol. The next event to be recorded shows that not all monks bore out Wycliffe's description of them as having 'red, fat cheeks and great bellies', and not all bishops could be fairly called the 'daughters of the diabolical leech'. William Canynges the younger was the head of a great and powerful Bristol merchant family, living in a splendid mansion behind Redcliffe Street. His nine ships, manned by eight hundred seamen, sailed the Bristol and English Channels, and the North, Irish and Baltic Seas. His fellow-citizens made him Mayor five times, and the imagination boggles at the number and size of the banquets over which he presided. But his heart was not in them, or went out of them when his wife Joan died. When that happened in 1467 he renounced his mercantile and civic life. In seven months he had been ordained and made a Canon of Westbury, and fourteen months later he was Dean of the College there. And so he remained in austere fulfilment of his vows until his death five years later.

He had been generous in his gifts to his own parish church, St. Mary Redcliffe, during the time of his business activity, and just before he left the pleasures of the world he endowed a chantry, St. George's Chapel, in the church, so that priests could say Requiem Masses for his wife's soul in Purgatory, and for his own and those of King Edward IV and Queen Elizabeth Woodville when they died. For he believed, in common with nearly all Christians of his time, that in this way the time that they spent in the place of purification could be reduced and their arrival in Heaven brought nearer. But he made yet more munificent gifts to Westbury College when he joined its ranks, making possible the rebuilding of the canons' quarters and the chancel of the church.

Not everyone was pleased by his generosity. He had apparently promised to his son John, though not in a legal document, that on his marriage with Elizabeth Middleton of Stanton Drew he would be provided with an ample income during his father's lifetime and with his lands and houses at his death. But William Canynges proceeded to give away a large portion of his wealth and reduce his own income to £33 a year. There was little for John and Elizabeth Canynges during William's lifetime; there was going to be a very small inheritance when he died. John asked the Lord Chancellor to force William to fulfil his promises, but while the matter was still unsettled John died. This is not the first or last time that a family has been upset by the generosity of one of its members to good causes outside the family, and the rights and wrongs of the case can still be argued.

The moving spirit behind the clerical career and later benefactions of William Canynges was John Carpenter, Bishop of Worcester. He had decided, like his predecessor Giffard, that his diocese needed a second Cathedral Chapter in Westbury, so that the pastoral needs of the largest town under his supervision could be more adequately carried out. He had better reason for this idea than Giffard, for Bristol was much larger and more important than it had been two centuries earlier. On the analogy of the Bishop of Bath and Wells he called himself Bishop of Worcester and Westbury, and enlarged the status and the buildings of Westbury College, with the help of Canynges, accordingly. We must hope and believe that

A Guild procession in the Middle Ages

he did not induce Canynges to take Holy Orders chiefly in order to avail himself of his wealth for Westbury. His idea of a double bishopric gained only local support, and his successor returned to the less splendid title of Bishop of Worcester.

We are drawing to the close of what are called the Middle Ages. New and revolutionary ideas were in the air of Europe, though they took some time to reach Bristol. Changes in the whole mental and spiritual atmosphere, and in the whole structure of society, were at hand. If we look at Bristol in the calm which came before the storm, we find a town of not much more than six thousand inhabitants, living on both sides of the Avon, and nearly all of them within the confines of the surrounding wall, their houses dominated and protected by the mighty Castle. There were a few rich families, who did themselves very well. There were many poor ones, who had to be content for the most part with cabbage, leeks, coarse bread and an occasional piece of meat. But there were many holidays, mostly on the Feast Days of the Church, and three times a year all the trade guilds in the town had a joint celebration called 'The Setting of the Watch', with a gaily-coloured procession, banners and torches carried aloft, dancing in the streets and free wine for all.

Bristol even then was a city of churches, fifteen within and just outside the walls, and one of them, the Chapel of the Assumption, among the houses straddling Bristol Bridge. Outside the walls were the monasteries and friaries, built there for the sake of seclusion and the regular performance of the sacred offices of the Church every day and night throughout the year. But the monks and the friars mingled frequently with the people in the streets, and many of them did parochial duties.

It is the modern custom to pour scorn on the religion of the Middle Ages. It is, of course, easy enough to point out the widespread superstition and ignorance, the striking contrast between the teaching of Christian love and the savage disregard of human life which characterized politics as well as war, and the equally striking contrast between the high professions of monks and clergy and the looseness of living which was sometimes to be found at the very heart of the

Church. We could certainly wish that the wisdom of the Church's thinkers and the holiness of her saints had been spread more widely among the ordinary people in every country. But religion for the man of those times had a quality which is entirely missing today: he believed that every part of his life was under the judgement of God and the watchful eye of the Church. The Church told him what was the just price to pay or to demand; the Church cared for him and his most serious interests at all the critical moments of life— birth, sickness, marriage, child-bearing, and death. If he broke, as of course he often did, the rules of the Church, he recognized the Church's right to reprove him and set him to do works of penance, to make up for the insult he had paid to God and the harm he had done to his fellowmen. We must be careful in our criticisms of him. For though we have a greater knowledge of science and the world in general than he had, and sometimes a better understanding of these things, we take away from God's control our work and games, and often more important things still, like friendship and marriage, and live, except when we are in church, as if God did not exist at all or had no interest in what we are doing.

CHAPTER 3

The Church Reformed

THE DATE of the beginning of the Reformation is usually
given as October 31st, 1517, when Martin Luther (1483–1546)
posted ninety-five 'Theses' (or topics for argument by learned
men) on the door of the Tower Church in Wittenberg in
Saxony. The Theses were about Indulgences. It was thought
to be within the power of the Pope to grant remission of sen-
tence in Purgatory to those who satisfied the conditions which
he laid down. These included repentance for sins committed,
and a money payment, and the remission was called an Indul-
gence. In 1517 a special series of Indulgences was being
issued all over Europe, and the money paid by those who
wished to reduce their time in Purgatory was used for the
rebuilding of St. Peter's Cathedral in Rome. Luther was
convinced that the Pope had no real right to grant these
remissions to operate after death; he thought that the whole
emphasis in the preaching of the Indulgences was on the
money payment, not the repentance that was also officially
required, and that the whole thing was becoming a sordid
swindle, battening on the superstitions of simple people. But
he was worried about something even more serious than this.
He had come to the conclusion that the whole system of
religion as the Church was teaching it depended on the idea
that a man could earn, or buy, the forgiveness of God by
doing good deeds—going on pilgrimages, adoring relics of
the Virgin Mary and the saints, paying for Masses to be said
for his soul after he had died. He knew from his own life that
all attempts to earn God's favour, even by the most strenuous
self-denial (he was a monk, and a good monk, and he had
tried all this), broke down, and that the only thing to do was
to put one's whole trust in the mercy of God, who forgave

sinners out of His sheer love for men. He had found this laid down in the Bible, especially by St. Paul; he had tried it, and found it to be true.

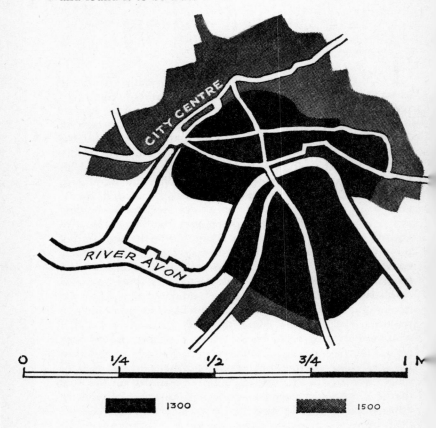

CITY CENTRE

RIVER AVON

| O | ¼ | ½ | ¾ | 1 M |

1300   1500

Bristol in 1500

So his protest against Indulgences broadened out into a full-scale attack on the teachings, and still more the practice, of the Church of Rome, and a bold attempt to reform it from top to bottom. First Germany, then all Europe, was in an uproar. Luther was expelled from the Church, and with the help of several of the great princes of Germany set up Churches on the principles which he had discovered in the Bible. He also brought out a translation of the whole Bible into German, so that everyone could read the Bible for himself, and Luther's German Bible has had as much influence on the history of Germany as the Authorized Version has had on ours.

Luther's movement of reform set others going in other parts of Europe. In Geneva, in French Switzerland, John Calvin (1509–64) set up an entirely new sort of Church—new, that is, by the standards of the time, but, according to Calvin, based squarely on New Testament principles. He cut out, not only the Pope, but bishops, maintaining that there is only one kind of minister mentioned in the New Testament, and that all ministers are of equal status. He also gave the members of his Church a part in the government of the Church, and set up a body of people, ministers and laymen, called the Consistory, to look after the private lives and conduct of all the people in Geneva. He worked out all the doctrines of the Christian Faith in logical form in a book called 'The Institutes of the Christian Religion', and included among them one which has caused endless argument—the doctrine of predestination, which says that God chose some people for salvation and some for damnation before the beginning of time.

There were other Reformers who were more drastic even than Calvin, and made Luther seem positively conservative (as indeed he was in several respects). Zwingli in Zürich, in German Switzerland, denied that the Body and Blood of Christ were in any sense present in Holy Communion, though Christ was present in spirit to those who had faith. Then there were some groups of people, called 'Anabaptists' by their enemies (but they themselves rejected the title), who said that the Bible ought to be carried out to the letter, and that therefore the Church should have nothing whatever to do with the government of the country and that no one ought to be baptized until he was old enough to decide for himself

The pistle off paul
Unto the Hebrues.

The fyrst Chapter.

God in tyme past diversly and many wayes / spake vnto the fathers by prophetes: but in these last dayes he hath spoken vnto vs by hys sonne / whom he hath made heyre of all thynges: by whom also he made the worlde. Which sonne beynge the brightnes of his glory / and very ymage off his substance / bearynge vppe all thynges with the worde of his power / hath in his awne person pourged oure synnes / and is sytten on the right honde of the maiestie an hye / and is more excellent then the angels / in as moche as he hath by inheritaunce obteyned an excelleter name then have they.

For vnto which off the angels sayde he at eny tyme: Thou arte my sonne / this daye begate I the? And agayne: I will be his father / ād he shalbe my sonne. And agayne when he bryngeth in the fyrst begotten sonne in the worlde / he sayth: And all the angels of god shall worshippe hym. ...th: He maketh his an̄sters flammes of fyre. ...th: God thy seate shal

A page from *Tyndale's Bible*
in Bristol Baptist College

(whether they understood the Bible correctly is another matter). Some of these Anabaptists were wild men and cranks, who brought ill fame on the others, but most were sober people who only wished to live the Christian life as they understood it in peace and quiet, and were hardly ever allowed to do so.

All these explosive ideas came, of course, to England, and were furiously discussed, especially in the University of Cambridge. One of the group of scholars who met there to hammer out the truth was William Tyndale, perhaps the most brilliant scholar of them all, though he was trained in Oxford and did not belong to the group for very long. He was entirely won over to the Lutheran position, and began to preach about it in many places. He was a Gloucestershire man, and for a time was children's tutor in the manor house of Little Sodbury. From there he came to Bristol, and preached the new doctrines on College Green, right in front of the Abbey of St. Augustine. No doubt there was a furore, but, if so, it soon died down. Yet Bristol had now heard for the first time the notions that were splitting the Christian world asunder.

Tyndale now conceived the idea of translating the Bible into English as Luther was putting it into German, and went to the Bishop of London, Cuthbert Tunstall, for support. Tunstall refused to give it, and Tyndale spent the rest of his life abroad. He finished the translation in 1525, but it was banned in England, partly because it was equipped with notes on the text which expressed Reformed doctrine in a powerful form and criticised the Pope very bitterly. Tyndale himself was hounded down by his enemies, and finally betrayed, strangled and burnt. But his translation lived on, and formed the foundation, both in its scholarship and its great literary beauty, for all future English versions. An almost complete copy of his New Testament is in the library of the Bristol Baptist College.

Henry VIII during the first part of his reign had no truck with any of the new notions. In fact, he wrote a book to show how wrong Luther was, and was greeted by the Pope as Defender of the Faith. But he was very impatient with the constant demands that the Pope was making on the by-no-means ample resources of his realm, and not at all pleased to have his powers curtailed by the decisions of a foreign prince, even if that prince was the living representative of St. Peter. So when he became sincerely doubtful whether his marriage to Catherine of Aragon had really been sanctioned by God, since their male children were apparently fated to an early death, and the Pope nevertheless, for purely political and selfish reasons, refused to declare it null and void, and when he badly wanted to marry Anne Boleyn in order to have an heir to the throne, he was ready to shake England free of Papal control. Once he had made up his mind, and found in Thomas Cromwell and Thomas Cranmer the willing instruments of his purpose, he acted with lightning speed. Between 1529 and 1539 the Church and realm of this country became completely independent, spiritually and financially, of the Church of Rome, and the links of a thousand years were broken; the monasteries were dissolved, the Bible in English was put in every parish church; and Henry became the Supreme Head of the Church of England. But it must always be remembered that Henry never gave any countenance to Reformed doctrine (except for a brief flirtation with some Lutheran doctrines when it suited his book to be on good terms with the German Protestant States). He was to the end of his days a Defender of the old Faith—to the great discomfort, and sometimes ruin, of those who thought that separation from the Pope ought to mean separation from all his errors as well.

The rising town of Bristol could not be kept out of these great matters, for the opinions of its leading Churchmen and citizens were beginning to carry weight outside its own boundaries. Matters were brought to a high pitch of excitement by the preaching of Hugh Latimer (1485–1555). Latimer was one of the group of Reformers who had studied together in Cambridge; he was also probably the greatest preacher of the age in England. Because of his eloquence he was appointed by the University of Cambridge as one of twelve preachers who were entitled to preach anywhere in the country, and he was soon popular as an orator at Henry's court. But he gave vent to views of a Protestant kind which brought him into trouble with the authorities soon after he had become Rector of West Kington, in Wiltshire, and he was brought to trial. He retracted his dangerous statements, and was restored to his position. Then he set out for his parish, and a little while later Archbishop Warham, who had acted as something of a brake on Henry's zeal to sever himself from Rome, died, and was succeeded by Thomas Cranmer, who was wholeheartedly with the king. So Latimer knew that he could now come out with his real views again—he had never, in fact, changed his mind about them—and appeared in Bristol, which was in the same diocese as his Wiltshire parish, in the spring of 1534, to preach in St. Nicholas' and St. Thomas' Churches in the city, and in the chapel of the Dominicans. In his sermons he asserted that the Virgin Mary was not sinless, but needed to be saved by Christ like all other members of the human race. He decried pilgrimages and honouring the images of the saints, as leading to superstition. And he aroused a great deal of anger by claiming that the souls in Purgatory were in Christ, and therefore did not need Masses to be said for them. The money spent on having Masses said for the dead could, he maintained, be better used in repairing dangerous roads, and in providing for poor men's spinster daughters, for the unemployed and for the sick.

It was clear that Latimer was now saying again the things which he had solemnly retracted, and he was speedily suspended from further preaching. His opponents made sure that powerful champions of the traditional opinions should appear in Bristol pulpits in the next few weeks. Among them was John Hilsey, Prior of the local Dominicans, Edward Powell, a noted scholar, and Hubberdin, a very popular preacher. Hilsey was soon entirely won over to Latimer's point of view, and supported him strongly. Hubberdin made the most impression on the public. He was eccentric in the pulpit and out of it; a few years later he leaped about in a pulpit so violently that it collapsed, and he broke his leg.

He never recovered from the injury, and the churchwardens of the church which witnessed his fall excused themselves on the ground that they had made their pulpit for preaching, not dancing. Powell showed the greatest determination of all Latimer's opponents, and continued the struggle for many

Hugh Latimer preaching

years. In the end he was executed for loyalty to his convictions, having refused to take the oath acknowledging the Act of Succession or to admit that Henry was the Supreme Head of the Church of England.

After the initial setback, Latimer in Bristol carried all before him. His enemies carried their attack on him to the length of saying things against the King, and it was revealed that the Dean of Bristol, John Floke, had given secret instructions to the clergy not to pray for the King and his new Queen, Anne Boleyn. This was enough for a royal order to be sent, setting up a commission, consisting of three ex-mayors, the Abbot of St. Augustine's and some other local dignitaries, to look into the disturbances which had broken out in the town. The charges against both Latimer and Hubberdin were heard, and judgement given solely against Hubberdin, who was put in prison.

Latimer was now high in the King's favour, and in 1535 was appointed Bishop of Worcester. His diocese was enormous, and although Bristol was the largest centre of population within it, it could not expect very long or very frequent visits from its bishop, especially as he was expected to sit in Parliament and carry out many tasks for His Majesty. But we may be sure that whenever he did come to Bristol the strife which he had kindled in previous years broke out again. The Dominican Friars ranged themselves on the bishop's side, the Franciscans fought against him, and even when the bishop was not in Bristol his name and his views were flung backward and forward with unabated vigour. Latimer, so far as his political duties allowed him, was a good and faithful pastor of his people, anxious to look into and redress any form of social injustice brought to his notice, and living in great simplicity himself.

His episcopacy of four years saw the two great changes in the religious life of this country which showed ordinary people that the religious conflict raging from time to time in various places was not just the result of yet another quarrel (they had happened often) between the Pope and the King of England which would soon be cleared up, but the beginning of a new age and a new direction of affairs. The first of these two changes was the Dissolution of the Monasteries, the smaller ones in 1536, the larger ones in 1538 and the following years. None of the Bristol monasteries, friaries or nunneries were particularly important, wealthy or corrupt. On the contrary they seem to have been sparsely populated and

3

quite ordinary at the time of the Dissolution. The Dominicans, as we have seen, had already tended to side with the King's party, and the Abbot of St. Augustine's had been a member of the commission which had vindicated Latimer againt Hubberdin. So there was no great resistance to the Dissolution, and no popular outcry against it. In fact, several of the houses surrendered their property of their own free will, and neither King nor Church made much money out of the business. Yet the sudden disappearance of the monasteries, and of the familiar figures of monks and friars and nuns, meant a break with the immemorial past which must have made a deep impression on the mind of every Bristolian.

The other great change was the appearance of a Bible in English in every parish church. This was ordered to happen in August 1537, but it probably took place over a long period. The version used was a combination of Tyndale's with that of Miles Coverdale, who borrowed a great deal from Tyndale, but wisely left out Tyndale's Lutheran notes in the margin and his ultra-Protestant translations of certain words. Perhaps only a few learned and well-informed men reflected, when they first saw the English Bible in their church, that it was only a few months previously that Tyndale had been strangled and burned in Flanders for the crime of translating the Bible into English. But Tyndale's dying prayer had been answered: 'Lord, open the King of England's eyes'.

Latimer was well aware that his diocese was far too large for one bishop to handle, and was authorised in 1538 to appoint Henry Holbech, who had been Prior of Worcester, as Suffragan, or assistant, Bishop of Bristol. But when Holbech went in 1541 to be Bishop of Rochester, Henry changed his mind about Bristol, abolished the Suffragan Bishopric and included the town in the new diocese of Gloucester. Bristol pride was just attempting to recover from the shock when Henry changed his mind again, and Bristol at last became a fully-fledged city with a Bishop and Cathedral of its own.

The Bristol diocese was an odd affair. It comprised the city of Bristol, some neighbouring Gloucestershire villages, and the greater part of Dorset; the last-named area was cut off from the other two by a wide corridor of countryside belonging to the diocese of Bath and Wells.

The first Bishop was Paul Bush, who had been the Prior of a dissolved monastery. Henry was thus saved the expense of paying a pension to a displaced Prior, and by economising on the endowment of the see obtained a bishop on the cheap. The provision of a cathedral was not on a very generous scale either; St. Augustine's Abbey was of course used for the purpose, but its church had fallen into grievous disrepair in the last half-century, and the nave had been recently pulled down. Little money was provided for its repair, and for three hundred years Bristol Cathedral consisted of half a church. So few people, for several centuries to come, wanted to be Bishop of Bristol, except as a stepping-stone to higher things.

Latimer resigned the Bishopric of Worcester in 1540, and so lost his connexion with Bristol. This was after Henry had decided to put a stop to further developments in the direction of Protestantism, and issued the Six Articles, the 'whip with six strings' for lashing the Protestants. Latimer was in prison for a while, and then retired into obscurity. Just before Henry's death he was put in the Tower of London, but Edward VI's accession released him and restored him to a place of prominence and influence, as one of the preachers at the court. But when Mary came to the throne, he was sent back to the Tower, then degraded and burned in Broad Street, Oxford. It was he who said to Ridley at the place of execution: 'Be of good comfort, master Ridley, and play the man. We shall this day light such a candle, by God's grace, in England, as I trust shall never be put out.' He was old and rather feeble by the time of his death, and there is a pathetic reminiscence of his Bristol triumphs in the description of his walk to the scaffold: 'after Ridley came Master Latimer in a poor Bristol frieze frock, with his buttoned cap and a kerchief on his head and a new long shroud hanging over his hose and down to his feet'.

The regents of Edward VI—he never became old enough to make his own decisions—pressed on the Protestant Reformation of the Church of England with great speed—some would say, with indecent speed. The Duke of Somerset was sincere, moderate, sensible and tolerant—far too much of a gentleman for those harsh times. The Duke of Northumberland was no sort of a gentleman; he was aggressive, ruthless, completely selfish, and a glutton for power. Among the measures of Somerset's time was the dissolution of the chantries, and the consequent abolition of Masses for the dead; and the issue of the first English Prayer Book. Cranmer was largely responsible for the form and the language of the latter, and he had prepared the people for it by having some parts of the Latin Mass said in English from the beginning of Edward's reign. When the Prayer Book appeared, it was wholly in English, and the Mass was now a service of Holy Communion in which the whole congregation was encouraged to take an active part. We can easily imagine how strange the services must have sounded in churches which had rung with the Latin language for so many centuries, and how those who disliked change, especially in religion, must have bitterly complained. The men of Cornwall rose in rebellion against the new order, on the ground that, while the sound of Latin was at least familiar to them, they could not understand English at all. But Bristolians accepted things without too much demur.

The Duke of Somerset did not treat the rebels of Cornwall and other places with enough brutality to satisfy the Earl of Warwick (soon to become the Duke of Northumberland), and he was put out of the way. Reformation for Northumberland meant mainly the robbing of churches by confiscations of all sorts. But Cranmer brought out a new Ordination Service, a second Prayer Book more Protestant than the first, in which certain services were compulsory for all Englishmen to attend, and the Forty-two Articles (later reduced to the familiar number of Thirty-nine).

The Reformation in England had now gone about as far as any reformer had any right to expect for the present, and too far for many Englishmen. Northumberland's methods, however, had created more social and political than religious discontent. The money from the chantries (some of them very richly endowed) was not spent on education, as had been promised, but on filling national and personal coffers. The plate from the monasteries, churches and chantries in Bristol was partly confiscated by the Corporation, melted down, and turned into money to buy monastic property, such as the chapel of St. Mark's Hospital, which is still owned by Bristol and known as the Lord Mayor's Chapel. Much of it went to the friends of the chief courtiers. The rest went to the Crown. It was ordered to be melted down to make money for the country's financial needs. But Sir William Sharington, from 1546 Treasurer of the Bristol Mint, had other ideas for the plate which came under his control. A Sharington shilling came to be worth about threepence; the value of the remainder was in Sharington's pocket. He was caught and tried, but, since he was able to give information that was useful to the Government, he was allowed to live for the rest of his life in comfortable retirement in his handsome ex-nunnery at Lacock.

Mary's reign was popular until the full extent of her fury against the Protestants was known. If the speed of reform was too fast for English people in Edward's reign, the extent of reaction in Mary's reign was too much for them to stomach at all. Yet Bristol, which must have contained a large number of Protestants, if we may judge from its previous history, did not provide a very large number of Marian martyrs. So far as can be told, four or five laymen were burnt, near the spot in Cotham where Highbury Chapel now stands (one Roman priest had been burnt in Edward's reign). Perhaps Bishop Holyman, Bush's successor, was mild in his enforcement of the anti-heresy laws. Perhaps the Bristol merchants felt that there had been enough interruptions of commerce already, and discouraged undue religious zeal, in order to carry on 'business as usual during alterations'.

When Elizabeth I entered on her reign in 1558 she made it her first concern to bring unity to the nation by making peace in the Church. She set about doing this by restoring the Church to the position in which it had been in the first part of Edward VI's reign, and by announcing herself to be its Supreme Governor. The Prayer Book of 1552 was made compulsory, and the clergy when conducting worship were instructed to wear such vestments as had been in use in the year 1549. It was, of course, laid down in the Prayer Book that laypeople should receive both the Bread and the Wine in the Communion Service. It was expected that Christian people would bow when the name of Jesus was uttered in church, and kneel during prayers. The clergy were ordered to do far more teaching and preaching than they had been in the habit of doing. They were allowed to marry, but only after the bishop and two Justices of the Peace had given approval to the lady selected.

About two hundred clergy in the whole country were not willing to accept the new order, and had to leave their livings. The rest acquiesced, some with a better grace than others, some with enthusiasm. There was more difficulty about the bishops; almost every one of them had been appointed by Mary, and could scarcely stay in office under her successor. So Elizabeth had to find two Archbishops and a whole bench of bishops.

It was soon quite evident that her purpose was to include within the Church of England everyone who could be persuaded to stay, and to do so by striking a course between Roman Catholic teaching on the one side and the views of extreme Protestants on the other—the 'middle way', as it was called, between Rome and Geneva. It was the kind of compromise which is dear to the heart of every ordinary Englishman, who strongly dislikes all extremes, either in politics or in religion, and suspects a great display of zeal, even in a good cause. It was certainly dear to the merchants and churchmen of Bristol, and probably to the great majority of ordinary citizens as well. After so much quarrelling and change, peace and order were good things in themselves, and could be ensured by the simple process of going regularly to the dignified services of the parish church; if one had views which did not exactly tally with those of the Queen and her bishops, well, it was just as well to keep them to oneself. So it was in Bristol, and over most of the country, for the greater part of Elizabeth's long reign.

When we think of the growing prosperity, founded on skilful trading, of Bristol as a mercantile city in the period of the Reformation, and also of the intelligence needed to keep up with and understand the rapid changes in the life of the Church—sometimes baffling to the clergy themselves—it is natural to ask how Bristolians received their education. The answer, of course, is that most of them received none, except what was available at home. Before the Reformation all the schools that existed were under the direct control of the Church. There was one connected with St. Augustine's Abbey, which was dissolved with the Abbey, and refounded as the Cathedral School when Bristol received its bishopric. There was another at Westbury, which probably disappeared when Westbury College was disbanded. Perhaps some of the chantry priests had a few pupils—that was quite a common arrangement in many parts of the country. This, of course, ceased in the reign of Edward VI. Fortunately a new school was founded in Henry's reign which did something to fill the gaps that were made—Bristol Grammar School, which took over in 1532 the buildings of St. Bartholomew's Hospital, which was no longer fulfilling any useful purpose. The founders were two prosperous merchants, Robert and Nicholas Thorne, who traded largely with Spain; they wanted to see that merchants' sons were properly trained to take their fathers' places in building up the city's trade. But something went wrong with the foundation very near the beginning. The Corporation was appointed by the founders to govern the school; in 1561, when both the founders were dead, it allowed the lands attached to the building, which were intended for the school, to go back into the hands of the Thorne family, no doubt after some money had passed from the family to the Corporation. Some of the land was given back to the school in 1617 by a decision of the High Court in London.

Queen Elizabeth's Hospital was founded by the will of John Carr, soapboiler in a large way. He asked for the school to be run on the same principles as Christ's Hospital, then in St. Paul's Churchyard in London, and now in Horsham, Sussex. That is why the boys of Queen Elizabeth's Hospital wear 'blue coats' to this day.

If a Bristolian had left the city in about 1520, travelled in foreign parts for many years, and returned home in, say, 1565, what changes would he have noticed in the church life of his birthplace? He would have seen no monks or friars in the streets, and the houses which they had inhabited when he left either falling to ruin or (more often) changed into parish churches or put to other uses. Inside the churches the chantry chapels would have been changed, often, into family pews for the rich. On the walls, instead of paintings of the saints or the Holy Family, he would have seen the Lord's Prayer and the Ten Commandments inscribed. In place of the old stone altars which he remembered from his youth he would have seen wooden tables that were moved into the body of the church for Holy Communion. If he attended the Sunday services, he would have found that the Mass said in Latin no longer took the most important place—in fact, he would not have been able to hear a Latin Mass in any church anywhere in the city, unless he happened to overhear some old priest, who could not get used to the new ways, mumbling parts of it to himself in the intervals of the service he was supposed to be conducting. In its place were services said in English which gave a great part to the reading of the Bible and the preaching of the sermon, followed once a month in the morning by the Holy Communion, in which the elements were carried round to the people as they sat or stood around the Communion Table. He would have seen the clergy robed very differently in different churches, some with surplice and cap, some with surplice only, some with neither—and some with a square cap, some with a round cap, some with a button cap, some with a hat. In some churches he would have heard a sermon thoughtfully put together and clearly delivered; in others he would have heard some ill-educated half-peasant monotonously reading one of the Homilies (sermons published by the Church authorities) which he probably did not understand himself.

For Elizabeth's Church of England, though governed by an Act of Uniformity, was by no means uniform; and thirty years of Reform had not abolished all the old abuses.

CHAPTER 4

The Church Divided

As the reign of Elizabeth went on, several groups of people became more and more unhappy about the religious situation. Those who preferred the Roman Catholic form of Christianity were, of course, unhappy all through. At first many of them went to the parish church, and so kept the law; and at home received the Sacrament of Holy Communion from Roman priests kept in hiding for the purpose. Others did not attend the official worship at all, refusing to have anything to do with such a wicked ordering of the Church, and gave constant trouble to the authorities. Both of these groups of people were called Recusants, and there were some in the neighbourhood of Bristol, as elsewhere. But Elizabeth was careful not to come down on them too heavily, and so outward peace was maintained. Then in 1570 the Pope excommunicated Elizabeth, that is, declared her to be right outside the Christian Church and unworthy to receive its Sacraments, and announced that none of her subjects need obey her. This made all Roman Catholics into suspected traitors, and as such they suffered heavily for the rest of the reign, 280 of them being put to death. It was at least as much a matter of loyalty to the Crown as of religious belief, especially at a time when the very existence of England was threatened by the Roman Catholic powers of Europe. When the Spanish Armada was defeated in 1588, the danger from Roman Catholics became much smaller, and the Queen could hope for religious peace within her borders.

But this was not to be. The later years of the reign were disturbed by the first rumblings of the religious storm which was to divide the country in bitter conflict. The full-blooded followers of John Calvin, who are called Presbyterians in the

English-speaking countries, had accepted the Elizabethan Settlement, but not with joy. In fact, they had done so in the hope that in a few years' time it would be possible to reform the Church more completely, and bring it really into line with Calvin's ideas. But the years passed, and the Queen showed no sign of encouraging or allowing any further changes. Meanwhile in the churches the Presbyterians had to watch rites and vestments—in fact, often actually to perform the rites and wear the vestments—which they connected with the old, bad times of Popery. So their loyalty to their bishops wore very thin, and in the end, in many cases, vanished completely. A large number of them came together secretly to form an underground movement. Underneath the surface of ordinary parish life a 'consistory' of ministers and laymen was to meet, to deal with those who lived bad lives or taught false doctrine; groups of twelve consistories were to assemble every six weeks in what was called a 'classis', and representatives of twenty-four 'classes' were to meet in a 'provincial synod' every six months, with a national meeting of synod representatives once a year. This was not carried out in all areas by any means, and was really powerful only in East Anglia. But it was very dangerous to the established order throughout the Church of England, for it meant that a popular movement might be worked up to drive out the bishops, and a Presbyterian organization would be already in existence to take over the whole Church—much as Communists are organized for their own purposes in non-Communist countries.

When these facts came to the notice of the Archbishop of Canterbury, Whitgift, he acted quickly and ruthlessly: the 'classes' were wiped out of existence, and the leaders were imprisoned. Yet the Presbyterians still nursed their beliefs in secret.

None of this seems to have had any effect on Bristol, except that the news of it helped to prepare the ground for what was to come.

There were other groups of Protestant Christians who were not willing to stay inside the Church of England at all, even

in the hope of improving it by secret planning; they thought
that such a hope was a waste of time. The first to put their
views on paper was Robert Browne (1550–1633), an eccentric minister who was imprisoned several times for his beliefs,
went for refuge to Holland, came home, re-joined the Church
of England, and finally—no doubt because of the persecu-
tions of his early years—went out of his mind.

In a book written when he was still young and vigorous,
called 'A Book which showeth the Life and Manners of all
True Christians', Browne said that the teaching of Christ
about the Church was summed up in His words, 'Where two
or three are gathered together in my name, there am I in the
midst of them'. From this Browne drew the conclusion that
the true Church of Christ was 'gathered' out of the world,
and consisted of people who had personally given themselves
to Christ and formed a congregation of His 'saints'. Each of
these congregations was to be independent of every other
one (hence the names given to Browne's movement, at first
'Independency', and later 'Congregationalism'), and sub-
ject only to Christ Himself. 'When two or three are gathered
together in Christ's name, He is one of the company, and
their acts are His acts.'

From this it is easy to see what Browne and his followers
thought about the Church of England, which was con-
trolled by the Queen and consisted of everyone in the land
whether they were real Christians or not. He had a very low
opinion of the bishops, too, and compared them with the
scribes and Pharisees as described by Christ in St. Matthew's
Gospel, chapter XXIII. He refused to stay in such a Church
ruled by such bishops, and formed a 'congregation' in
Norwich in 1581. This led to his imprisonments, and he decided
to take his congregation and himself to Holland, where they
would be allowed to worship as they thought right. Another
congregation was founded by Henry Barrow in London, and
Parliament passed an Act against 'seditious sectaries'. As a
result, Barrow and others were executed. After Elizabeth's
death the Independents began to come back to England and
establish their churches here, but a large group preferred to

go to America; in Plymouth they joined up with a group of harassed Independents from England who were about to make the same journey, and so the voyage of the *May-flower*, followed by that of several other ships on the same errand, provided America with the most famous of its pioneer settlers (1620).

The adventures of the Brownists have taken us beyond the age of Elizabeth, who died in 1603. When James I succeeded her, the Puritans, as the Protestant opponents of Elizabeth's measures had come to be called, had high hopes of at last moulding the Church to their pattern, for James had been brought up as a Presbyterian, in Scotland, home of the true Reformed Church. But James soon dashed all such hopes and set himself against the men who had cherished them. 'No bishop, no king', he said, and meant it. He knew himself to be king of England and Scotland by divine right, and who were these grim-faced ministers (he had had enough of their sort in Scotland) to tell him how his Church should be run? He probably did not realise how strong the Puritans were becoming in the Church and nation, and thought that a few well-chosen words from the throne would soon put them right. If so, he was certainly mistaken.

Near the beginning of his reign a new kind of English Independency showed itself, but in Holland, so that he only heard of it some years later. John Smyth (1554–1612) was the pastor of an Independent Congregation first of all in Gainsborough, and then in Amsterdam. But he decided that the Independents had not really worked out their own beliefs to their proper conclusion. 'Since the Church, as Browne has shown, is the gathered congregation of believers, and since the way into the Church, as the Bible plainly teaches, is through Baptism, it surely follows that only believers should be baptized; the baptism of infants is not baptism at all!' So he re-baptized himself (or, as he would have said, baptized himself for the first time), and set up the first congregation of English Baptists in Amsterdam in 1608. One of his most trusty followers was Thomas Helwys. But the two men later disagreed about some items of their faith (not baptism), and

Helwys came back to form the first Baptist congregation in England, in Spitalfields, London, in 1612. Helwys later published the first full, reasoned argument for 'toleration', that is, for allowing men to worship God as they chose and for keeping the State out of a man's personal relations with God. In fact, we owe to the Independents and Baptists the final success in England of the idea that every man has a right to hold and practise his own faith, so long as he does not interfere with the freedom of others. But their time was not yet; they had to endure many years of bitter persecution before the nation accepted this idea.

James I may perhaps sometimes have had some doubts about the doctrine of the Divine Right of Kings, or at least about pressing it to extremes in the face of opposition. His son, Charles I (1625–49), had no doubts at all on either point —in fact, he was faithful unto death to his belief. When his Parliament criticised his policy or aired its grievances, it was, to his mind, acting against God; its proper business was to carry out the king's wishes and raise the money for the purpose. The members of Parliament, on the other hand, were equally sure that the duty of protecting the interests of the people whom they represented, and of asserting their right to worship according to their consciences, was laid upon them by God. Here was a clash of deeply and sincerely held religious beliefs, and its climax was the Civil War. Many other matters of dispute helped to cause and continue the war. But at the heart of it lay a religious issue, and we do well to remember that on both sides there were sincere and God-fearing men.

For eleven years, from 1629 to 1640, Charles governed without any Parliament at all. During this time William Laud, first as Bishop of London and then as Archbishop of Canterbury, carried out the king's wishes, which were also his own, in Church affairs. Laud's enemies said that he wished to bring the English Church back to the Roman one. But this is not so. He wanted the Church of England to be exactly and in all respects what Elizabeth, James and Charles had commanded it to be, and he therefore insisted that every

Englishman and Englishwoman should do in church exactly what the Prayer Book and the royal instructions told them to do, or suffer for it. He had a consuming passion for reforming, at once and thoroughly, everything that lay within his range, and that included the whole Church. Sober, faithful bishops and clergy, who approved of all that Laud believed in, were mercilessly scolded and punished for breaking a rule, and not even the members of his own party had any love for him. But it was the Puritans, of course, who suffered most, and it is not surprising, though hardly fair, that they came to call him 'the great and common enemy of all goodness and good men'. Yet he was just and honest, and utterly loyal to his convictions; it was only that he lacked imagination, sympathy and a sense of humour. He was the first of Charles' henchmen to suffer death for the king's cause.

In Bristol the last years of Elizabeth and the early years of James were years of religious peace. But in 1613 William Yeamans was appointed Vicar of St. Philip's, and he was a man of strong Presbyterian views. He conducted the services in the parish church as the Prayer Book laid them down, but he forbade the worshippers to bow at the name of Jesus and had hard words for anyone whom he saw breaking the Sabbath. And on weekdays he held services in other places than the parish church—in the house of William Listun, a glover, in Lawford's Gate, and in that of Richard Langford, a carpenter, who lived in the grounds of the Castle, among other places. He and his devout flock were safest in Langford's house, because the Castle grounds were legally in Gloucestershire, not Bristol, and the Bristol magistrates on the warpath had no hold over them there. At these private services there was free prayer, and much preaching from the Bible—'prophesying', as it was called. We cannot tell how big the congregation was, but it certainly made up in zeal what it lacked in numbers, for it went on meeting after Yeamans' death in 1633, and invited various ministers from South Wales to come and preach from time to time.

Most people, as usual, were quite content with the services in the Cathedral and their parish churches, and these no doubt went quietly on. In 1630 Bishop Wright raised £568 to adorn the Cathedral with its statues of prophets and evangelists, and in 1634 three visitors from Norwich remarked that the eighteen churches of the city were 'fayrely beautify'd, richly adorned, and sweetly kept'. 'In the major part of them', the report goes on, 'are neat, rich and melodious Organs that are constantly play'd on. Their Pulpitts are most curious, all which the Citizens have spared no cost nor forwardness to beautify and adorne (a pious and religious example for all our Kingdome).'

The wealth which rich citizens before the Reformation had lavished on chantries was now being spent, evidently, on the adornment of parish churches, and some of it went to the founding of schools. John Whitson, who had grown rich in the Spanish trade in 'Bristol Milk', left money in his will for the provision of a boarding school for forty daughters of dead or poverty-stricken Bristolians. He died in 1629, and the school was set up in 1634; the Red Maids received their distinctive costume at the very beginning of the school's life.

The Bristol clergy must have been disturbed by the doings of Yeamans and his friends, but they were too busy, at any rate in the sixteen-thirties, trying to carry out the instructions of Archbishop Laud in their own churches, to bother very much with the 'prophesyings'. But if they hoped that they would die out, they were disappointed. Exactly the opposite happened soon after the arrival of Matthew Hazzard, a young and enthusiastic Puritan minister, in the city. After serving for a time in various churches in a minor capacity, he became Vicar of St. Ewins. His preaching had already gained a following of people with Puritan ideas, including Dorothy Kelly, the widow of a grocer in High Street, Anthony Kelly, who had been a member of Yeamans' congregation. Mrs. Kelly had zealously kept up her Puritan habits after the deaths of her husband and of Yeamans, even to the length of keeping her grocery shop open on Christmas Day, to show that she was not the victim of superstition (for the Puritans refused to keep any holy day except Sunday, and they thought that Christmas, as it was kept in those days, was a pagan beanfeast). It was thought by many of the Puritan group that Mrs. Kelly would make an excellent wife for Mr. Hazzard, and he came to the same conclusion. She agreed that it was the will of God, and they were married.

Mr. Hazzard's views were not so strong or extreme as his wife's. He was quite content to use the Prayer Book in his parish church, though he showed his Puritan sympathies by refusing to give Holy Communion to all and sundry who happened to come to church. This was not enough for his wife. She wholly disapproved of the reading of prayers in church, and was in great conflict, because she thought it was her duty to attend the services conducted by her husband. In due course she and her friends decided to take a middle course by coming into church soon enough to hear the sermon, but too late to hear the prayers. Meanwhile she was forming a group of 'true believers' around her, which met in her house during the first part of the morning service in the parish church, and then again on Sunday afternoon. A few months later she decided that her conscience did not allow her even to hear the sermon in church, and so the group stayed away from that. Her enemies were rather pleased about this, for they thought it would cause a quarrel between her and her husband, and so make a scandal which would ruin her cause. But this did not happen. Husband and wife agreed on many points, but not on that of separating from the Church of England, and there they agreed to differ.

The small group of people meeting in Mrs. Hazzard's house for prayer, preaching and Bible study, under the leadership sometimes of Robert Bacon, sometimes of Mrs. Hazzard, became a 'separated' congregation, fully organised. This was in 1640, and by the time the Civil War began in 1642 there were about a hundred and sixty members. Out of this group came Broadmead Baptist Church. It was not at first a Baptist Church at all, but 'Independent', though some of those who preached there were of the Baptist persuasion. A similar group was also meeting in Filton before the war broke out. Meanwhile a little company of Baptists had started to meet in the Pithay, perhaps before the foundation of Broadmead.[1]

The Civil War made many quick changes in the official religion of the nation. In 1644 the whole system of bishops, together with the Prayer Book, was abolished, to make way for Presbyterianism. This was made compulsory in England, and led to the departure of many clergymen from their livings; others were already of Presbyterian views, or now adopted them, and stayed on. Oliver Cromwell changed all this. He looked upon his 'New Model Army' as a 'congregation' of true Christians called by God to set the country in order. When he had defeated and executed the king, and become Lord Protector, he set out to reform the religion, as well as the government, of England on Independent lines. He gave a much wider measure of toleration than either Charles I or the Presbyterians had done, but not to Roman Catholics or Anglicans; and the intrusion of his officers into the private life of Englishmen steadily aroused great discontent. Only a minority in the country ever became Puritan, and the great majority welcomed Charles II home from his travels soon after Oliver's death.

The Puritans in Bristol had a bad time at the beginning of the war, once Bristol had fallen to Prince Rupert in 1643.[2] Many of the Puritans made their way to London, accompanied by their friends from South Wales who had previously taken refuge with them from the king's officers. But just over two years later Rupert was driven out by the Parliamentary forces, and the evacuees came back. The Roundheads expelled from office the leading men in the city who had supported Rupert, and sold Bishop Howell's park and palace over his head; the lead was stripped from the roof of the palace in spite of the fact that Mrs. Howell had just given birth to a baby. Mrs. Howell, and later the Bishop, died from the effects of this brutal treatment.

[1] It later became Old King Street Baptist Church, now in Redland.

[2] Mrs. Hazzard and her friends sent a large store of provisions into the Castle for the siege, and barricaded the Frome Gate with woolsacks when Rupert approached.

The Puritans at last were free to worship as they pleased and where they pleased, and their numbers grew into thousands. It is actually recorded that the Mayor of the city signed a letter inviting Mr. Ewins to come from South Wales to be the pastor of the Broadmead congregation. But trouble of two sorts was in store. A fierce argument broke out among the members about the rights and wrongs of infant baptism, and many of those who rejected it left Broadmead to become members of the Pithay Baptist congregation; some of those left in Broadmead were Independents, some Baptists, with the proportion of Baptists steadily increasing (though Broadmead did not become purely Baptist for another two hundred years). The stauncher Independents were, however, free to go to the recently founded Independent Congregation on Castle Green.[1]

The other sort of trouble was caused by the Quakers. The founder of the 'Religious Society of Friends', as the Quakers should properly be called, was George Fox (1624–91), an outstanding religious genius. A Leicestershire man of no education, he became very dissatisfied with all the Churches, and could find no peace or truth anywhere until he was convinced that 'the light which lighteth every man' (referred to in John 1. 9) would give him all the truth he needed. By this he meant that everyone of us has an 'inner light', a light from God Himself; if we nourish that light, it will guide us in all things, telling us what to believe and what to do.

Armed with this discovery he set out on foot to reform the religion of England in 1647. He had no use for churches (which he called 'steeple-houses'), or ministers ('hirelings'), or sacraments ('idolatry'), and his attacks on them led him into serious trouble. He was prosecuted sixty times, and spent six years of his life in prison. But his positive teaching about the need to obey the light that is within us, together with his striking personality and great eloquence, gained him many followers—50,000 of them, it is said, at the time of his death.

The first Quakers to come to Bristol were John Audland and John Camm from Westmorland in 1654. They preached

[1] Now in Greenbank.

first of all to the Independents and Baptists already meeting outside the parish churches, and also to the 'Seekers', little groups of people looking for a more personal kind of religion than the Churches seemed to offer. Audland and Camm won many followers, but greatly annoyed the Broadmead Independents by taking away about a third of their number, including one of their leaders called Dennis Hollister, who served in one of Cromwell's Parliaments. They annoyed the parish clergymen even more by the things which they said about the services, and things were made much worse for them by the strange behaviour of one of the leading Quakers in the West of England, James Nayler. Nayler was a sober and sensible man, very sincere and brave. But in 1656 he was returning from a preaching tour in the West country, and reached Bristol to find a party of Quaker women waiting for him at Temple Meads. Carried away by enthusiasm, they shouted out 'Holy, Holy, Holy, Lord God of Sabaoth', and Nayler, instead of telling them to be quiet, allowed them to escort him noisily into the city. Such moments of weakness may come to anyone, and Nayler was bitterly sorry afterwards; he was also severely punished by the Commonwealth authorities. The Quakers of Bristol at once reproved the women who had behaved so badly. But the rumour went round Bristol that Quakers were people who did wild and blasphemous things, though of course they were not, and many years passed before it was lived down.

The Quakers had a Meeting House in Broadmead, and George Fox made it the base for many of his operations in the West. In 1669 he was married there to Margaret Fell; they spent their honeymoon in Bristol and Olveston, and then parted to go on preaching tours in different directions. In 1670 the Quakers of Bristol bought the house of the Dominican Friars in Rosemary Street, and this, under the name of Quakers' Friars, remained the chief Meeting House of the Bristol Quakers until after the Second World War.

In 1660, with the accession of Charles II, the tide turned violently against the Puritans. Charles and his advisers were determined to have no more division in the nation on the matter of religion, and by a series of Acts, known as the Clarendon Code, he commanded all his subjects, on pain of imprisonment, to attend the services according to the Prayer Book in the parish churches, and made it illegal to worship anywhere else; Puritan ministers who refused to conform

A Quakers' Meeting

were forbidden to go within five miles of any place where they had previously worked. Later Acts made it impossible for anyone who refused to go to Holy Communion in the parish church to hold any office in military or civil life. Those who refused to conform were called 'Nonconformists', or 'Dissenters', and formed quite a large minority up and down the country. Charles, in his effort to unite the country, had made permanent its division into two.

Life was very grim for the Dissenters in Bristol during the reign of Charles II. They were not persecuted for every moment of the time. They spoke of ten periods of persecution, with short intervals between them. There was even an interval of a few months when they had a royal licence to meet and their preachers had a royal licence to preach. But they never knew when they would be pounced upon and carried off to Bridewell for short terms of imprisonment. Their ministers were liable to much worse things than that —six months in a filthy jail, and sometimes an early death there from the appalling conditions.

Yet they carried on with their services regardless of the dangers. They met mostly in private houses, only to be ferreted out by informers who received good wages from the city authorities, with the warm support of the bishop. They tried worshipping in the open air, so that they could quickly disband when their scouts gave warning of the approach of the informers or the militia, but they were often caught and imprisoned none the less. The Baptists made it a practice to hold services in the woods of Hanham and Kingswood, and in Brislington and St. Anne's near the banks of the river Avon. The river served two purposes: it was used for baptisms by immersion, which is the Baptist practice, and it was a way of escape. For across the river was another county, Gloucestershire, and the Justices of the Peace there were not quite so keen on hunting down Dissenters. But on one unfortunate occasion the Baptists were meeting on Brislington Common when the Justices' men came on the scene. The congregation scattered; some were arrested, others reached the river and were ferried across to Crew's Hole—only to meet the troops of the Gloucestershire Justices, who on this occasion had joined in the chase. In the scurry and flight that followed one Baptist was drowned, and a preacher from Taunton was nearly drowned and died later.

The Quakers suffered more than the other Dissenters. This was to be expected, for they had refused to take the oath of allegiance to Charles II on his accession, on the ground that Christians should not swear oaths at any time; and they were so sure that services in the parish church according to the Prayer Book were wrong and superstitious that they had no hesitation in disturbing them with loud protests even at the height of persecution. Besides, they had a habit of going through the city clothed in sackcloth—'as a sign', they said, that it would shortly be destroyed by God as a punishment for its sin. None of these things made them very popular with their fellow-citizens.

The chief enemy of the Dissenters was Sir John Knight, who described their meeting houses as 'prattling boxes', and suspected them of joining in anti-Royalist plots which certainly had some Bristol supporters. When he was mayor from 1663–4 the Dissenters had the worst time in their history in Bristol. But it should be added that Knight was also very unpleasant to the Cathedral authorities, whom he tried hard to cheat on financial matters; and it would seem that in his later years he grew more reasonable in his attitude. Ralph Carleton became Bishop of Bristol in 1674, breathing fire and brimstone against the Dissenters. He led a police raid on Quakers' Friars in 1679, and haled a number of the Friends to jail.

But some good came out of much evil. One of the leading members of Broadmead Chapel for thirty years until his death in 1679 was Edward Terrill, an Almondsbury man who was a member of a prosperous business firm and also came into much property through his marriage. He was a 'scrivener', that is, he drafted documents for business and legal purposes, and he was also expert in Hebrew, Latin and Greek, and a man of some social standing. He used a great deal of his wealth to help his fellow-Dissenters, by paying their fines and in other ways; and he wrote down a faithful account—not without some severe disapproval of the beliefs and worship, as well as the behaviour, of Anglicans—of the early days of Broadmead Chapel and the hardships which fell on its members. It is to his 'Records of a Church of Christ' that we owe most of our knowledge of Bristol Nonconformity in these troubled times. His will provided that the money from the sale of his property should be used for the maintenance of 'a holy, learned man, well skilled in the tongues, viz., Greek and Hebrew', who was to instruct young men three half days in the week and prepare them for the Baptist ministry; there was also provision for scholarships for the young men if they needed them. The terms of his will, after some delay, were carried out in 1720, and from that

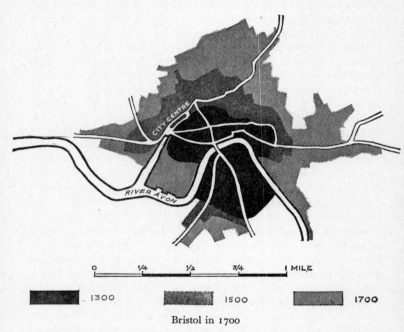

Bristol in 1700

time 'Bristol Baptist College', as it came to be called, has sent a constant stream of trained men into the Christian ministry, many of them to work in the Church overseas.

In St. Mary Redcliffe Church is the tomb of Sir William Penn, the Bristol admiral who captured Jamaica from the Dutch in 1655. His eldest son, also William, became a Quaker in 1665, and when his father died in 1670 he went to Charles II, reminded him of a debt of £16,000 owed by the king to his father, and asked, not for the repayment of the money, but for a grant of land in the New World where he could build up a colony. Charles saw the double advantage of discharging a debt and getting rid of a number of Quakers at one blow, and granted him land which was to be named Pennsylvania in honour of his father. Penn established the colony on Quaker lines, with freedom of worship for all and without any appeal to force. He was dismissed from his post as Governor of Pennsylvania by William III, and became a wandering preacher in England. In 1696 he was married to Hannah Callowhill in Quakers' Friars; his wife continued to preach, though she became the mother of seven children. Penn returned to Pennsylvania for a period in 1699, and his statue still stands on the summit of the City Hall in Philadelphia, with his arm stretched out over the city, though the city itself retains little of the simplicity of life which Penn recommended.

Charles II's death in 1685 brought his brother James II to the throne, and James proceeded in 1687 to announce toleration for all. Some of the Dissenters, including William Penn, thought that he was going to bring in a new age of religious peace, and then discovered that his real aim was to restore the Roman Catholic faith. So when many parties united to force the king out of the country and bring William III and Mary to the throne, there was for a short time an alliance of Anglicans and Nonconformists to defeat a common foe. This was carried further by the Act of Toleration in 1689, which allowed Dissenters to meet in their own places of worship so long as the buildings were duly licensed as Dissenting Chapels and the trustees guaranteed that the ministers taught the doctrine of the Trinity. This did not mean that all restrictions on Dissenters were removed. They were still not able to hold office in nation or city, and the Test and Corporation Acts which barred this were not repealed until 1824, though yearly Acts were passed during most of the eighteenth century to exempt them temporarily from these laws. In other words, they were still second-class citizens, and the tragic division of the nation into two parts, which had been caused by the

Civil Wars and made lasting by the Clarendon Code, was by no means at an end.

It is a relief to record that since the sixteen-eighties no one has had to die for his faith in Bristol. Christians at last came to realise that the cause of Christ is never served by hounding Christians of other convictions than their own to prison, exile or death. The persecutors on all sides—and scarcely any part of the Church which has had sufficient power in its hands to persecute has a clean record—sincerely believed that their opponents' views were undermining the Church of God and often the government of the country as well, and they believed so passionately that their own views were right that they could not rest until they had destroyed all trace of the others. Now we can see that God's truth does not need to be protected by violence, but only by sincerity, faith and Christian living. But we are in danger of giving 'indifference to the truth' the name of 'Christian toleration', and claiming credit for what has no value at all. We can rightly criticise the men of the sixteenth and seventeenth centuries only if our convictions are as strong and sincere as theirs.

CHAPTER 5

The Church Revived

IN 1700 BRISTOL was the third city in England to London and Norwich, with a population of about 27,000, and was steadily moving up into second place. But the streets and buildings of the city were scarcely worthy of its importance. There was an average of twenty feet between the houses on either side of the streets, with rough blocks of stone to form the carriageway and no pavement to protect the pedestrian; down the middle ran an open channel where the pigs rooted among the garbage, while the slops were poured into it from the overhanging houses of plaster and timber. The roads leading into the city were not much better; Queen Anne, travelling from Bath in 1702, found the road impassable. But there was plenty of trade and traffic in the streets, and therefore much congestion; John Wesley was once thrown off his horse and nearly crushed against the wall by a cart coming in the opposite direction.

As the century went on and Bristol became richer and richer, many of the meaner areas vanished, the centre of the city was rebuilt, and handsome squares and streets appeared, lined with dignified houses for the prosperous merchants. Kingsdown and the Marsh (now known as Queen Square) were the most favoured areas, and the Pump Room at Hotwells drew fashionable visitors who believed that they could obtain relief for ulcers, diabetes, gout and rheumatism, and be seen in the company of the right people at the same time.

The Church all over England was exhausted by the religious quarrels of the preceding century. The Church of England had not only lost the Presbyterians at the Restoration, and the Independents and the Baptists before that; at the accession of William and Mary four hundred clergy and six bishops (including Sancroft, Archbishop of Canterbury, Lake of Bristol and Ken of Bath and Wells) found themselves compelled by their consciences to refuse to take the oath of allegiance to the new sovereigns; they had sworn to obey James II, and he was still alive. So they disappeared from the life of the Church, and the Church was much poorer for their going. Many of the clergy and bishops left behind were determined to preserve at all costs the position which they had won from the Puritans at such expense of life and danger, and the reign of Anne (1702–14) witnessed several attempts to put Dissenters back in the place from which the Toleration Act had rescued them. In 1711 the Occasional Conformity Act enacted severe penalties against those who 'occasionally conformed', i.e., went to Communion at the parish church now and again to qualify them for civil and military office, while remaining Dissenters at heart; but the Schism Act of 1714, designed to close down all the schools and 'academies' (or colleges) run by the Dissenters, was never put into effect because of the death of Queen Anne.

The coming of the House of Hanover and the long control of Parliament by the Whigs induced the Church of England to accept things as they were. Ambitious Churchmen saw the advantage of forming an alliance with the party in power. When a man of this kind wanted to become a bishop—and most of the bishops were of this kind for most of the eighteenth century, though there were shining exceptions—he agreed to support the Whigs in the House of Lords on the virtual promise of a wealthier bishopric later on. The bishops had to spend seven or eight months of every year in London, in order to attend the House, and some of them did not visit their dioceses even in the remaining months. The clergy were often infected by the same disease of ambition, or by laziness if their ambitions came to nothing, though there were, as ever, many faithful pastors (who were not well known, because they simply carried on with their work in their parishes). The parishes were all too often held 'in plurality'; that is, one man drew the income from several livings, and the actual work in all the parishes except one was done by an ill-educated, underpaid and half-starved curate, while the Rector kept himself well in with the local gentry. Meanwhile thinking people were casting great doubt on the truth of the Christian faith, and saying that by using the power of reason every man could find out all that he needed to know about God and the world; and few Christians had the skill or the power to defend their faith against its enemies. So there was a very cold wind blowing through the Church of England, and the ordinary man and woman did not find that it offered them much help and comfort, especially if they lived in the dirty and crowded towns that were being rushed up near the factories, the mills and the mines, far too quickly for clergy to be provided for their spiritual welfare.

There was one thing, too, that the bishops and clergy could not stand at any price, and that was 'enthusiasm'. The word had a special meaning in the eighteenth century—the kind of religion which claims direct information from God and shows itself in acts of worship outside the ordinary run. Genuine 'enthusiasm' in this sense is, no doubt, a dangerous thing, since it gives people the idea that they have a private, exclusive knowledge of God's will. But the trouble was that the Church authorities tended to label any serious, personal religion by the evil name of 'enthusiasm'.

While so many clergy and laymen of the Church of England slumbered, the Dissenters were not very wide awake either. They, too, were exhausted by the harsh struggles of the preceding century, and they wished to enjoy their partial, but hard-won, freedom in peace and quiet. They were mostly thrifty and hard-working citizens, and some of them were very successful in business. They made, however, a big contribution to higher education. The two Universities of Oxford and Cambridge, the only two Universities in the land, were closed to them. Therefore they ran their own 'academies', which were colleges for the training of ministers and of all Dissenters who wished to enter the professions. After the attempt to close them down at the end of Anne's reign had failed, they went from strength to strength, and probably reached in many cases a higher standard than that of the Universities; also they had a wider curriculum which included the sciences, at a time when most people limited education to the ancient languages and mathematics.

As the century wore on some of the Dissenters lost not only their zeal, but their belief in some of the articles of the Christian faith as it was taught by the Church at large. Quite a number of Presbyterian and Independent Churches, and a few Baptist ones, became Unitarian, that is, they ceased to regard Jesus Christ as God, and thought of Him only as a very good and inspired man; they felt that to call Him God meant believing in more than one God, and they wished to preserve the 'unity' of God (hence their name).

The Quakers, as usual, had their own history. They dropped the rather noisy preaching and protests of their early years, and concentrated on cultivating the spirit of quiet worship which is typical of the Society of Friends; at their meetings no one speaks or prays until he feels himself led by the Spirit to do so, and a whole hour may pass without a spoken word from anyone. But they also had two other interests: business, at which they often excelled, and the service of their fellowmen. They were always in the forefront of charitable work, and played an especially large part in the movement against slavery towards the end of the century.

Things in Bristol were no worse and no better than they were anywhere else. But there were some events to enliven the general dullness of religion there during the first part of the century. Edward Colston (1636–1721) was born in Bristol and lived nearly all of his life away from it, engaged in great overseas trading enterprises which required his presence in London. And even when he came towards the end of his business career he lived in Mortlake, not in Bristol. But he had a great love for his native city; absence seems to have made his heart grow fonder. He gave an almshouse on St. Michael's Hill to the city in 1690, and rebuilt and increased the Merchants' Almshouses in 1695. In the same year he increased the number of free scholars at the City School by six. He wished to increase it by many more, but the Corporation would not accept the conditions which he laid down. So in July 1710 he by-passed the Corporation and founded an entirely new school, handing it over to the Merchant Venturers to control. There was a master, two assistants, one teacher of the Catechism, and a hundred boys. So Colston's School came into existence. He also helped to rebuild Temple Colston School, then a charity school for poor boys, and gave money to the Temple Church, All Saints, St. Mary Redcliffe, St. Werburgh's and the Cathedral.

It is very suitable that so many Bristol streets, buildings and institutions should be named after Colston, because of his great generosity. But he was not an easy man from whom to receive gifts. He was always very careful to lay down very strict rules as to how the money was to be spent. He was a 'High Churchman' in the sense in which those words were then used—he thought that the rights and exclusive position of the Church of England should be preserved for ever. So no Dissenters' sons were allowed at Colston's School, nor could any boys from either of his two schools be apprenticed to Dissenters; nor were any books used at Temple Colston School to have any trace of Whig ideas on politics or religion. Church attendance was, of course, compulsory for all his boys.

As Bristol spread during the century far beyond the city walls, Dissenting chapels sprang up here and there, in Brislington, Kingswood and several other places. The Independent Congregation in Lewin's Mead became Unitarian in 1775, when it had a famous minister, John Prior Estlin, who also kept a private school. The Baptist College grew and prospered; under the terms of Edward Terrill's will, the minister of Broadmead Chapel was always its head, and in the eighteenth century Caleb Evans was the most distinguished of those who held the double office. The Quakers were small in number, meeting in Quakers' Friars, Temple Street and Frenchay, but, in Bristol as everywhere else, large in influence and charity. Apart from many gifts of money, often anonymous, to good causes, they backed the unique enterprise of Dr. Edward Long Fox, who in 1794 opened a mental hospital in Downend, and moved it to larger premises in Brislington in 1804. It really was a 'hospital', not a place for chaining up lunatics, which was the usual way of treating those whose minds were deranged. Fox believed in games, excursions and useful occupations for his patients, and so showed the way for the modern treatment of mental illness.

Bishops of Bristol followed each other in quick succession throughout the century, often on their way to some more splendid office. Their average stay was four years, and they could scarcely afford to stay any longer, for their stipend was so low (a mere £400) and their expenses so high. One who stayed longer than most, and did more for the city, perhaps, than any other, was Joseph Butler, Bishop from 1738 to 1750, when he moved on to the much wealthier see of Durham. He was brought up as a Presbyterian and educated at Tewkesbury Academy. Then he joined the Church of England, and went up to Oxford before being ordained. He soon became a famous London preacher, and gave great comfort to Queen Caroline, wife of George II, during her last illness. This probably helped his appointment to the see of Bristol; for part of the time that he was here he was also Dean of St. Paul's, and the income from this office was very useful when it came to paying for the many improvements he made to the inside of his Bristol Palace, especially in the form of stone and marble chimney pieces. He got an Act through Parliament which created the new parish of St. George's in the mining area of the city, showing that he was well aware of the needs of his own day, as well as being a great thinker and scholar.

The sermons and the book which have kept his name alive in the country as a whole were both produced before he came to Bristol. In his 'Fifteen Sermons' he showed that self-love, love of others, and conscience are the most important parts of us all, and that if we obey their commands we shall both be happy and please God; to give way to our passions and instincts is to destroy ourselves and others. In his 'Analogy of Religion' he is answering those who say that the beliefs of

Christianity cannot be proved like a proposition in geometry, and therefore should be abandoned. It is absurd, he says, to expect to prove religion like a theorem. We can show that Christian faith is probable, and that is quite enough, for probability is the guide of life.

Josiah Tucker was a curate and parish priest in Bristol from 1737 to 1790. He became Dean of Gloucester in 1758, but did not give up his Bristol living until nine years before his death. The parishes which he held were first St. Stephen's and later All Saints, and they both brought him into close touch with the leading merchants of the city. He was more of an expert on trade and commerce even than on theology. He wrote against monopolies (the holding of all the trade in a particular article by one firm) and high duties on the oil that was used for making Bristol soap; he was in favour of canals, taxes on bachelors and dogs, and on allowing the American colonies to be free from Britain. In 1780 he wrote a book in which he foretold that the American nation would one day 'make a most distinguished figure among the nations of the earth and in the history of the world; while the European nations are sinking into weakness, poverty and contempt'. Some of his books were so daring in their ideas that he would not let them be published until after his death.

In spite of these outstanding figures, the religious scene into which George Whitefield burst in 1736 and 1739 was a dull and drab one. Bristolians were busy, but not with their prayers. Whitefield (1714–70) was born in the Bell Inn at Gloucester, and at sixteen was a tapster in that establishment. But he went to Oxford, where he came to know the Wesley brothers. In 1735 at Oxford he suddenly found freedom, by trusting in Jesus Christ, from his worries and fears and temptations. He was ordained deacon, and began to preach. It was soon clear that he was no ordinary preacher. People complained that his first sermon, preached in Gloucester, had sent fifteen people mad; the Bishop of Gloucester, who had just ordained him deacon, replied that he hoped that they would not recover from their madness before the following Sunday. The truth was that Whitefield had a power of stirring people up which had never been known in living memory, and the effects of his preaching were so unusual and profound that it was natural to confuse them with madness. Wherever he preached the same kind of thing happened, and soon he was sure of a vast congregation whenever it was known that he was coming anywhere. He preached in Bristol in 1736, and was asked to do so on every day of the week while he was there. But he only stayed for a while, for he was on his way to Georgia. In that newly founded British colony he set up an Orphan House, which stands there to this day, and many of his travels were devoted to raising funds to keep it open. He could always count on a good collection. He came back to England to be ordained priest in 1739, and could not stop preaching while he was in the country. He returned to Bristol for a longer stay than before. The crowds were waiting for him in the churches. 'Some hung upon the rails of the organ-loft', we are told, 'others climbed upon the leads of the church, and altogether made the church so hot with their breath, that the steam would fall from the pillars like drops of rain.' But his success provoked jealousy, and the regular parishioners complained that the rag, tag and bobtail of Bristol were crowding them out of their pews in church. It became evident that Whitefield was soon going to be forbidden to preach in the pulpits of the city, and he anticipated this by preaching in the open air instead, a habit which he had learned in America.

He had heard of the savage and evil way in which the colliers lived in Kingswood Chase. They recognised no law and order, and no one dared to impose them. They lived in foul sin, and died in horrible squalor. That was what Whitefield was told, and he went to see for himself. The truth was not very different from what he had heard, and he began to preach the Gospel on Rose Green, first of all to two hundred, soon to four thousand, five thousand and more. And they believed his words; they had never heard before in their lives that God loved them, and when the news was brought to them by Whitefield they were overcome with joy and gratitude. Whitefield did not just preach, and then go away; he set about building a school for the colliers' children. But he was soon due to go to America, and in any case the work was growing beyond even his powers to cope with it. So he sent a message to his friend John Wesley in London, asking him to come and help.

John Wesley (1703–91) came from a background very different from Whitefield's. He was the fifteenth child of the Rev. Samuel Wesley, Rector of Epworth in Lincolnshire, and his wife Susannah. He was brought up strictly, but with great affection, mostly by his mother. He was at Charterhouse School, and then went on to Oxford. He became a Fellow (that is, a lecturer and tutor) of Lincoln College, and seemed to be marked out for a brilliant career as a clergyman-scholar. But at Oxford he became the leader of a small group of students who had decided that the way in which professing Christians lived was not nearly strict enough. So they vowed to spend an hour morning and evening in private prayer, to study the Bible together from six to nine o'clock every evening, to take Holy Communion once a week, and to pay regular visits to the prisoners in the foul prisons of Oxford. This was most unfashionable behaviour, and earned them many nicknames. The one that stuck was 'Methodists', though the Methodists of that group were very different from the Methodists later on.

The members of the Holy Club (as the group was also called) gradually left Oxford, and John and his younger brother Charles were invited to join the colony of Georgia as chaplain and Governor's Secretary respectively. They went out in 1735, hoping not only to turn the colony into another Holy Club, but also to convert the Red Indians in the neighbourhood. They completely failed to do either. The colonists were a rough-and-ready body of people—many of them just let out of debtors' prisons—and refused to obey the strict rules of religion which the Wesleys laid upon them; so the longer the brothers stayed the more unpopular they became. They were hardly allowed by the Governor to meet the Indians at all. So they returned to England very sorry for themselves, and well aware that the religion which had been very helpful in Oxford had been of little value in Georgia. John consulted one of the members of a group of German Christians in London, called 'Moravians' (he had met them on the ship going to America and in Georgia, and we shall meet them again), and was told that the thing that really mattered in Christianity was personal trust in the love and power of Jesus Christ. John knew that the German was right, and he longed to have this kind of trust for himself. After many months of distress, it was given to him on May 24th, 1738. Not everyone can give the date when he became a thorough Christian, but John Wesley could. He tells us in his Journal for that day: 'About a quarter before nine . . . I felt my heart strangely warmed; I felt I did trust in Christ, Christ alone, for salvation; and an assurance was given me, that He had taken away *my* sins, even *mine*, and saved *me* from the law of sin and death.'

By a strange coincidence his brother Charles had gone through the same troubles and come to the same kind of solution, and an entirely new chapter was opened in the life of both of them. When John, a few months later, received the message from George Whitefield inviting him to Bristol, he felt some reluctance to go—but went nevertheless. The first sermon he preached in Bristol was in a brickyard where King Square now stands, and it was preached in the open air. This was a thing that Wesley had never done before, and hoped never to do. All through his life he disliked doing it. A comfortable church with a dignified pulpit, and everything done according to the proper rules, were very much more to his taste. But he preached several thousand sermons in the open air, because that was the way, and often the only way, to gain a hearing from the people to whom he most of all wanted to speak—those to whom church services meant little or nothing.

From King Square he went on to Kingswood, and a few days later was left alone by Whitefield to continue the work among the colliers. A quite astounding thing happened. Wesley had a bigger effect on his hearers, and a more lasting one, even than Whitefield. He did not preach with the same

John Wesley on Hanham Mount

fire and movement and dramatic power; he spoke plain English in a clear voice, and everyone who was listening thought that he was speaking personally to *him*, and that he *must* listen. Among the simple people of Kingswood, standing on the slopes of Hanham Mount, the first effects were alarming. A man would start screaming out loud, in dread of what would happen to him if he did not become a Christian; then roll on the ground in a frenzy; and gradually 'come round', with a look of peace and joy on his face, when he realised that his sins were forgiven. Wesley at first thought that this sort of thing was a proof that God was helping him; but he came to see that it was just emotional excitement and took no notice of it; and soon it was not happening any more. Most of his hearers did not behave like this at all, but hearing of the love of God for the first time in their lives, and discovering that God loved *them*, and would forgive *them*, stopped swearing and fighting and getting drunk, and became quiet, sensible people who made it their business to meet regularly with their fellow-Christians to build up their faith and learn from each other the best way to live.

Whenever people took his teaching to heart, Wesley organised them into 'societies' for Bible study, prayer and conversation. Within a few months there were three societies in Bristol, as well as one in Kingswood—the first few of a vast number which sprang up all over England during the next fifty years.

The Bishop of Bristol, Joseph Butler, was not very pleased to hear about all this. It was all very much like that dreadful and dangerous thing, 'enthusiasm'. He asked Wesley to call upon him. 'Sir,' said the Bishop, 'the pretending to extraordinary revelations and gifts of the Holy Spirit is a horrid thing; yes, Sir, it is a very horrid thing. . . . You have no business here; you are not commissioned to preach in this diocese: therefore I advise you to go hence.' Wesley intended to do no such thing. He claimed that as the Fellow of an Oxford College he had a right to preach anywhere (here he was certainly wrong; he had a right to *teach* anywhere, but not to preach), and told the Bishop: 'My business on earth is to do what good I can: wherever, therefore, I think I can do most good, there must I stay so long as I think so; at present I think I can do most good here, therefore here I stay.' In the same spirit he wrote a few weeks later to a friend: 'I look upon all the world as my parish; thus far I mean, that, in whatever part of it I am, I judge it meet, right, and my bounden duty, to declare unto all that are willing to hear, the glad tidings of salvation.'

He soon decided that the societies of Methodists meeting in various parts of the city needed a building of their own. A piece of land near St. James' Church, in the Horsefair, was bought, and the stone laid for a building, though there was hardly any money available. But the Methodists subscribed willingly, and the 'Old Room' was soon built and paid for; it was not very well built, however, and was replaced in 1741 by the New Room, which still stands as it did then. Wesley used it not only as a preaching place and a meeting-place, but as a base for all his activities in the West of England. As the Methodist movement grew throughout the country, Bristol, London and Newcastle upon Tyne formed the triangle which set the pattern for Wesley's whole strategy of preaching and organisation. The second of the conferences to which he called his helpers took place in the New Room in 1747, and very many of the Annual Conferences of the Methodist Church have taken place in Bristol since that date.

So John Wesley's first visit to Bristol, lasting only a few months, sowed the seeds of many future developments. He came back many times. In fact he never failed to visit the city in any year before the year of his death, 1791, and the average time that he spent there every year was over a month. It is not surprising that so many of the things which are typical of Methodism were tried out for the first time in Bristol. Until Whitefield and Wesley came along it was the custom of the Kingswood colliers to spend Saturday evening drinking; but when they became Methodists they began to spend it in prayer instead. In 1740 Wesley organised this practice into a regular service, beginning at eight or nine o'clock and continuing until just after midnight. These were called Watchnight Services, now held only on New Year's Eve. The Society at the New Room was discussing in 1742 the best way to pay off the money that was still owing on the new building, and a certain Captain Foy suggested that the Society be divided into groups of eleven people, each under a leader who would collect a penny a week from them. This was agreed to, and Wesley soon discovered that the leader of a 'class', as it was called, was in a very good position for looking after his eleven class members, and could collect them together for Bible study and prayer, and for discussing the Christian life. So every Methodist Society was divided up in this way, and the Methodist 'Class Meeting' was born.

Charles Wesley spent longer in Bristol even than John. He came to help his brother in the early days, and from time to time afterwards. In 1749, after his marriage, he settled down in Bristol to look after the Society in the New Room, and continued in this work until 1771. In his house in what is now Charles Street he wrote a large number of the six thousand hymns which bear his name. He wrote too many, of course, but an astonishingly large number of them count among the best hymns in the English language, for Charles was not only a splendid preacher but also a real poet, who could use words that expressed the deepest feelings of the Methodists—and of all Christians. He was a faithful attendant at St. James; several of his children died young, and their tombstones are to be seen in St. James' Churchyard.

Another of John Wesley's Bristol helpers in the early days was John Cennick, who was one of the first laymen allowed by John Wesley to preach. Wesley was very doubtful for a long time about the wisdom of allowing this at all, but John Cennick was so gifted that he did not stop him. Others afterwards followed suit, and John Wesley came to see that it was one of the chief ways in which his message could reach great numbers of people. Even John Wesley could not be everywhere all the time! John Cennick was also for a short time the Headmaster of the school for colliers that Whitefield had started in Kingswood, but in 1745 he left the Methodists and joined the Moravians. These were in origin a group of

German Protestants in Moravia and Bohemia who were badly persecuted in those countries and found refuge in the estates of Count Zinzendorf in Saxony. The Count became the leader of the Church, known properly as 'the Unity of the Brethren', and it spread across Europe in small groups, and found its way to America. We have seen how the Moravians helped John Wesley when he was in trouble. They believed very strongly in personal religion, but Wesley thought (perhaps wrongly) that they were inclined to shut themselves off too much from the sacraments and regular worship of the Church, though he borrowed several of his practices (with alterations) from them. Cennick founded a Moravian Church in Bristol in 1748; it was finally established in 1755 and continues today.

It is well known that the Methodist Movement was even more successful in America than in England. Bristol had a small share in the extension of Wesley's work across the Atlantic. Most of the first American Methodists were immigrants from Ireland, but among them there was also an Englishman, Captain Thomas Webb, who had lost an eye and part of his right arm in battles against the French in Canada. He heard Wesley preach in Bristol in 1764, and from that time forward he was a vigorous Christian and a powerful preacher. He went off to America and stirred up the Methodists to build a chapel for themselves in John Street, New York, in 1768. It still nestles at the foot of the skyscrapers. When Webb finally came back to his own country he settled in Bristol, and was mainly responsible for the building of Bristol's second Methodist chapel, Portland, the 'Chapel on the Hill' (that is, on Kingsdown), in 1792.

In 1771, meeting his preachers in the New Room, Wesley called for volunteers to go and preach the Gospel in America. Among the five who responded was Francis Asbury, a blacksmith from a village outside Birmingham, aged twenty-six. A month later he set sail for America from Pill. For fifty years thereafter Asbury rode up and down the vast spaces of his new country, facing hardship, opposition and illness, preaching, praying, writing, organising. He was to America what Wesley was to England, and there is no doubt at all that he was one of the great formative influences in the growth of America as we know it. He covered more than a quarter of a million miles, mostly on horseback, and everywhere in his wake there grew up and flourished chapels, schools and compact communities of Christians devoted to the love of God and the service of their fellowmen. There were many others like him and after him, of course. When the adventurous spirits of America in the nineteenth century obeyed the injunction 'Go west, young man', the Methodist 'circuit riders' and the Baptist preachers went with them, and it is because of this that the Methodist and Baptist Churches are the strongest Churches in the United States of America.

John Wesley did not only look across England and across the seas for work to do. He also looked very carefully at the conditions of life endured by the people to whom he preached, and did what he could in every way to improve them. He made it his practice to visit the prisons in the towns which he visited, and wherever he went conditions were appalling. Bristol Bridewell and Bristol Newgate were among the worst prisons in the country. In Newgate in 1720 the majority of the prisoners died of an epidemic of gaol fever; yet when the disease broke out again eight years later no doctor was called in. One cell, seventeen feet in diameter and seventeen feet underground, housed thirty prisoners. Wesley wrote of the conditions which he found there on his first visit: 'Of all the seats of woe on this side hell, few, I suppose, exceed or even equal Newgate [in London]. If any region of horror could exceed it a few years ago, Newgate in Bristol did; so great was the filth, the stench, the misery and wickedness.'

The gaoler, John Dagge, had been converted by George Whitefield, but this fact did not make much difference to his treatment of the prisoners—until John Wesley talked to him. Then all the cells began to be cleaned out, work was given to the prisoners to occupy their time, their grievances were dealt with by the gaoler, and when they fell sick they were properly looked after. Unfortunately Dagge's successor went back to the old methods.

When Wesley visited Knowle in 1759 he found eleven thousand French prisoners-of-war living 'without anything to lie on but a little dirty straw, or anything to cover them but a few foul thin rags . . . so that they died like rotten sheep'. He soon had his congregation sending warm clothes, and the Corporation helped with mattresses and blankets. He often made appeals for the Bristol poor, without any distinction of religion; and in the last years of his life he encouraged the foundation of the 'Stranger's Friend Society' (still existing), which was expressly concerned with non-Methodists.

He also had many ideas for the treatment of the sick, and published a book called 'Primitive Physick', which contains rules for the treatment of nearly every known disease. In the days before doctors were numerous, this book helped many people to cure themselves, or rather to allow Nature to cure them. Some of the suggestions, though derived from the best medical authorities of the day, strike us as curious, such as that for pleurisy ('a plaster of brimstone and white of egg, spread upon brown paper'). But the emphasis on early hours, regular exercise, plain diet and moderation, was very useful and timely. In later books he recommends the use of the newly discovered force of electricity for various conditions, and so anticipated some modern methods. More practical still was the setting up in London and Bristol of Dispensaries for the free treatment of the poor. No doubt many of the methods there used were primitive, but poor people had nowhere else to turn; many were helped, and Wesley was able to assert that no one had died as a result of treatment given out in his Dispensaries.

But Wesley's biggest and most lasting social work was in education. He tried to educate everyone with whom he had anything to do. Probably he was the pioneer of good cheap literature for the people at large. He himself wrote numerous pamphlets, and published those of many other authors; cheap editions of famous books, edited by him, were often appearing. A great deal of the printing of all these was done for him by Bristol firms. But adults are more difficult to

teach than children, and it was on the foundation and maintenance of schools that he spent as much time and energy as
on anything else that he ever did. He took over from Whitefield the school at Kingswood for the sons of colliers, and soon
had one for their daughters as well, another one (a boarding
school) for orphan girls, and an adult school, all meeting in
the same building. He also opened a school in the Horsefair.
All these were really experiments for discovering the right
method for educating the young. The school for colliers'
sons continued until 1803, but by its side Wesley had started
a much more important project in 1748.

This was Kingswood School proper, a boarding school for
the sons of Methodists. Wesley was disgusted by many of the
things that went on in most of the boarding schools of the
time, and was determined to make his school into a 'Christian family'. He provided a very full curriculum of studies,
and wrote many of the text-books himself; hours were very
long (beginning at 4 a.m.); no boy was ever supposed to
be out of sight of a master (it is hard to see how this was
carried out); there were no holidays, a great deal of religion,
and no games. 'He who plays when he is a boy will play
when he is a man', said Wesley; and his brother Charles
wrote a hymn to express this idea:—

> Let heathenish boys
> In their pastimes rejoice
> And be foolishly happy at play;
> Overstocked if they are,
> We have nothing to spare,
> Not a moment to trifle away.

It is probable that this hymn was not sung with much enthusiasm by the boys of Kingswood School. In fact, it is hard to
see how any school could survive the incredibly harsh rules
that Wesley imposed. But Kingswood School did survive
them, and gradually modified them; it was limited to the
sons of Methodist preachers after Wesley's death (the limita-
tion was taken off in the nineteen-twenties), and removed
to Bath in 1851. It stands today as one of the leading schools
in the West of England. So Wesley's basic ideas must have
been sound, though their expression was peculiar.

It was in Bristol, too, that Wesley took the step which of all the things that he did most vitally affected the relations of the Methodists to the Church of England. He asserted to his dying day that Methodists were faithful members of that Church, and he instructed them to attend its sacraments and other services, and never to hold their own services at times which clashed with these. He thought of Methodism as a 'Society' within the Church of England. But the Methodists and the other Anglicans did not get on very well together. The Methodists thought that most of the clergy were idle and useless, and the members of their flocks not very different. The clergy and the majority of Anglicans thought that the Methodists were noisy and self-righteous—'enthusiasts', in fact. So John Wesley was kept out of most parish pulpits, and the Methodists were frowned on when they went to the parish church. Wesley denied that his followers were Dissenters; but in order to open a chapel he had to register it as a Dissenting Meeting House. If he did not do that, his Anglican opponents threatened to prosecute him. So he had to give way on this point. But he still thought himself a faithful Anglican.

Wesley was persuaded by a book which he read in 1746 that in the New Testament an ordinary minister and a bishop are the same, and that an ordinary minister therefore has the right to ordain other ministers, just as much as a bishop has. He was often tempted to ordain some of the Methodist preachers, but for a long time he refused to do so, in order to prevent a split with the Church of England. But after the War of Independence there were scarcely any ordained ministers in the whole of America, and the Christians there had virtually no chance to receive the sacrament of Holy Communion. Wesley asked the Bishop of London to ordain a Methodist for the purpose, and the Bishop refused. So in 1784, at No. 6 Dighton Street, Bristol, Wesley ordained two men to be ministers in America, and another man, Thomas Coke, already a clergyman, to be their Superintendent.

This meant that the Methodist Society was about to become the Methodist Church, whatever Wesley might say about it.

So it was a very sad event, for which both sides must take their share of the blame. The separation was not made official until 1795, four years after Wesley's death. Here also Bristol came into the picture. There was a great dispute in the New Room as to whether the Methodist preacher, who had not been ordained, had the right to administer Communion. The trustees, that is, the people responsible for the upkeep of the premises, said 'No'; the rest of the congregation said 'Yes'. Those who said 'Yes' left the New Room and began to build a new chapel in Old King Street. The quarrel spread among the Methodists all over the country, and the Conference of 1795, in order to make peace, ruled that a Methodist preacher, appointed by the Conference, could administer the Sacrament if a majority of the leaders of his flock wished for it. This was soon brought into effect in nearly all the Methodist chapels, and the Methodist Church was independent.

So revival led to a division, which it has so far proved very hard to heal.

CHAPTER 6

The Church Successful

IT WAS DURING THE YEARS which we have now reached, those at the end of the eighteenth century and the beginning of the nineteenth century, that the modern world as most people think of it was born. It is fairly true to say that until about 1750 England was a country which lived by agriculture, with most of its inhabitants in villages and small towns. Then a great change began and went on faster and faster; the factories multiplied with astonishing speed, the population did the same to provide the labour for the factories, and by 1800 the majority of English people lived in large, sprawling, ugly, ill-built towns, with no drains to speak of, no open spaces, scarcely any doctors or schools, working from an early age under dreadful conditions for appallingly long hours at miserable wages. The years from 1800 to 1850 are rightly called 'the Bleak Age'.

These conditions were not nearly so common in Bristol as they were in the Midlands and the North, and a visitor to Bristol might not have noticed such a vast change between 1750 and 1850. The city had its long-established businesses, and the factories which grew up like mushrooms were mostly fairly small. But the population grew from about 50,000 in 1750 to 68,000 in 1800, to 98,000 in 1820, to 120,000 in 1830, to 140,000 in 1840, to 158,000 in 1850; and by 1900 it had more than doubled to 330,000. We must unfortunately suppose that a very large number of these people spent all their lives in mean streets and poor houses.

There is good reason to think that the churches in Bristol never succeeded in bringing more than a small number of the workers in the new factories to the worship of God. When a census was taken in 1851 of all those who went to church on Sunday, it was found that not more than a third of the total population attended church with any kind of regularity. Probably there were more in Bristol who did so than in many other places, but even so it must have been less than half; and the half of the population that did go was made up of the people who were better off. There was not room in the churches or chapels for all the rest, and most of the seats were charged a rent which the majority of people could not afford; besides, they had not the clothes which they thought were needed for going to church, and felt very uncomfortable and out of things when they did pluck up their courage and go. Far more people went to church in the second part of the century than in the first—but the population had gone up, too, and even when the churches were at their most successful, in the eighteen-eighties, still less than half the people went to them. The rich people, and those who were not actually rich, but were yet quite well off, went to church in greater numbers then than ever before or since. But few of the workers went, and the boom in religion hardly touched them. So when we speak of the success of the Church—and we shall see that it was successful in many ways—we have to remember that many people were left right out of it, and that our century is not the first time that people have stayed away from church. It is more cheerful to remember that great numbers of the workers' children went to the vast Sunday Schools that flourished throughout the nineteenth century. They did not always stay very long, but they learned some of the first things about the Christian faith. But now we must go back a little to the earlier years of the nineteenth century.

One of John Wesley's greatest concerns in his later years was the campaign against slavery. For a time Bristol was at the very centre of the slave trade. The ships left the Port of Bristol with goods produced in the neighbourhood; these were exchanged for human cargoes in West Africa; the slaves were sold in the markets of the West Indies and America for work on the sugar and tobacco plantations; and the ships returned to Bristol laden with sugar, rum and tobacco, which were the price paid for the slaves. This triangular commerce was the chief secret of Bristol's growth in prosperity and population during the first half of the eighteenth century. From 1750 onwards the trade declined in Bristol, and grew correspondingly in Liverpool. It may be that Bristol consciences were aroused by the preaching of Wesley and others (he was not nearly so frequent a visitor to Liverpool), it may be that the ships required for the trade as it developed were too large for Bristol wharves. By the end of the century the Bristol trade in slaves had almost ceased.

Wesley became more and more thunderous against the slave trade in the seventeen-seventies and seventeen-eighties, and the last letter he ever wrote was to William Wilberforce, urging him to continue to the end his fight against 'that execrable villainy, which is the scandal of religion, and of human nature'. But Wesley's voice was by no means the only one raised in Bristol against it. Dean Tucker wrote and spoke in strong support of the anti-slavery campaign. The Quakers, here as everywhere (and especially in Pennsylvania), used all their influence on the same side. So when Thomas Clarkson, an Anglican deacon, came to Bristol in 1787 to investigate and expose the city's share in the horrible trade, he found, not only that its share had declined (though what was left was shocking enough), but that he already had many influential supporters.

The man who did more than any other one person to end the slave trade in the British Empire, and ultimately to abolish slavery altogether, was William Wilberforce (1759–1833), who was persuaded to take up the cause by Thomas Clarkson. Wilberforce gave up the chance of brilliant success in politics in order to serve the slaves, and he did so entirely because he believed that this was his Christian calling. He was greatly influenced by John Newton, once the captain of a slave ship, later the friend and protector of the poet William Cowper; he became Rector of a London parish and author of the hymn 'How sweet the name of Jesus sounds'. Wilberforce in later life settled in Clapham, then a fashionable suburb of London, and became the leader of a group of Anglicans called the 'Clapham Sect' (not a very good name, as they did not form a sect at all). The members of this group, and others like it in other parts of the country, were called 'Evangelicals'. They were impelled by the same kind of faith and zeal for preaching to those outside the Church as we have found in Wesley, and probably they owed much to him. But they differed from him in various ways: he believed that God's love was free for all, they were strict Calvinists, that is, they held (like George Whitefield, who had parted company from Wesley on the same ground) that God decided before the universe began who was to be saved and who was to be damned. Then they were not prepared to act outside the framework of the Church of England, and strongly disapproved of Wesley's method of sending preachers to live and preach for a year or two in one place after another.

One of the most prominent members of the Clapham Sect, especially in the last part of her life, was the Bristol lady, Hannah More (1745–1833). Born in Stapleton, she taught at a school opened by her sisters in Clifton. But she was invited to London because of her literary gifts, and was soon moving there in the circle of Edmund Burke, Joshua Reynolds, David Garrick and Samuel Johnson. She wrote poems, plays for the London stage, and, after she had been converted to a personal faith of an Evangelical kind, more serious works for the improvement of people's behaviour. She never abandoned her interest in the theatre. In 1787 Wilberforce and she were so shocked by the conditions under which the miners in the Mendips lived, and by their uncouth, immoral habits, that they determined to found schools in Cheddar and the surrounding villages. This was accomplished by the money of Wilberforce and the personal efforts of Hannah More. There was soon as great a difference in the behaviour and attitude of the Mendip miners as Wesley and Whitefield had made in Kingswood. She lived for a long time in Blagdon, and then in Barley Wood in Wrington (there is a long epitaph to her in the church there), writing many pamphlets and doing many services to the poor. She was sure that God had arranged for some to be rich and powerful and others to be poor and weak, but she thought that the rich ought to help the poor in every possible way. This does not strike us as very advanced thinking, but it was quite novel to many rich people in those days. When she was eighty-two years old she came back to Clifton with a great reputation as a Lady Bountiful, and lived in the midst of her friends and admirers for another six years.

One of the evils that troubled the Evangelicals was the fact that while the rich could get the education they needed, the poor had very little chance of doing so. We know what Hannah More did in Somerset; in other places Sunday Schools were part of the answer. Robert Raikes of Gloucester is usually credited with having invented Sunday Schools. This is not correct. What he did was the very valuable work of organising and extending the Sunday Schools that already existed. There was a Methodist Sunday School, for instance, in Almondsbury in 1778. Raikes began his great drive forward in Gloucester in 1780. The first purpose of Sunday Schools was to teach reading and writing, so that the children could read the Bible for themselves. It was out of the basic ideas of the Sunday School that day schools for the children of the not-so-rich developed. Early in the nineteenth century Dr. Andrew Bell started Anglican schools, which came to be called National Schools; Joseph Lancaster, the Quaker, started schools in which the religious teaching was not that of any particular denomination, and these came to be called British Schools. Sad to relate, the two kinds of schools were often conducted in deadly rivalry with each other, and the conflict between them made it impossible to open schools for all the children of the nation until 1870. But their presence meant that Sunday Schools were able to limit themselves to instruction in the Bible, and the other subjects were taught in the day schools. Some of the schools both of Bell and Lancaster were built in Bristol, and the Bristol Sunday Schools in all denominations grew rapidly all through the nineteenth century.

The Evangelicals, for all their zeal, were never more than a select minority within the Church of England, and for the first part of the nineteenth century the main stream of Bristol Anglican life flowed on as placidly and muddily as ever, with few of the evils of pluralism and idleness removed. In the eighteen-twenties the movement for reforming the Constitution of England was getting into its stride. But the rich men of Bristol did not want Reform; nor did the Bishop, or most of the clergy. They thought that the system by which voting for Parliament was limited to those who owned their houses, and two Members of Parliament might represent thirty voters, while the great majority of the population had no representative at all, was quite satisfactory. Nor did they wish the superior position of the Church of England over the Dissenters and Roman Catholics to be altered. So when on Guy Fawkes Day, 1828, Prebendary Sydney Smith preached in the Cathedral a powerful sermon in favour of religious toleration, he had a very frosty reception from his hearers and the other important people in the city. But the tables were tragically turned on them in the Bristol Riots of October 1831. By this time the Reform Bill, designed to give the vote to a far greater number of the people than had ever had it before, had been passed by the House of Commons and thrown out by the House of Lords—which meant that it could not become law. The Bishop of Bath and Wells and the Bishop of Bristol—in fact, all the bishops—had voted against it. When the Bishop of Bath and Wells came to consecrate St. Paul's Church by the New Cut, he had to face a hostile crowd. But he went away unhurt. A few days later Sir Charles Wetherell, Recorder of Bristol and a violent opponent of Reform, came to Bristol. There was some rioting on a Saturday afternoon, and there was a threat to burn the Council House, but it was thwarted by the soldiery. Sunday morning was fairly quiet; Bishop Gray of Bristol preached in the Cathedral, and left the city soon afterwards. Trouble really started in the afternoon and early evening. The crowd attacked the Bishop's Palace, next door to the Cathedral, and burned it to the ground. The subsacrist, Phillips, barred the way to the Cathedral and saved it. Before the day was out, the Mansion House, the Custom

House and many private houses had gone, and there was feasting for the rioters in Queen Square. When the military restored order the following day, damage amounting to more than £300,000 had been done.

These disturbances, and smaller ones in other parts of the country, convinced King William IV and the House of Lords that the Reform Bill must go through, and in 1832 it became law. Bristolians had shown an ugly hatred for the Church and the Government which is without parallel in the city's history.

This was an over-rough awakening of the Church authorities, and did little good to the religious life of the city. The real stirring of life came when John Keble, on July 14th, 1833, preached his famous Assize Sermon in the church of St. Mary the Virgin in Oxford. He was worried because Parliament, having reformed itself, was beginning to reform the Church of England, the Irish part of it in particular. He thought that the Church should be free to order its own life in its own way; for it was part of the great Catholic Church of the centuries, guided by the Holy Spirit, and governed by Bishops in succession from the Apostles. And now Parliament was treating it as if it were just a human institution like any other, or like the 'churches' of the Dissenters! From this fiery protest grew a movement to bring back the Church of England to its true faith and practice, believed by the Oxford Reformers to have been more and more corrupted since the Reformation. Many Anglicans thought that the Tractarians, as they were called, were trying to lead the Church of England back to Rome—it is true that some of its leaders, notably the greatest of them, John Henry Newman, did become Roman Catholics—and there was much dispute everywhere; but the general effect of the Tractarian, or Oxford, Movement was to improve the services in the Church of England beyond recognition, and to produce clergy and bishops many times more sincere and keen in the exercise of their duties than the Church of England had known for a long time, except in Evangelical circles.

Bristol perhaps had less than its proper share of these good results of the Movement, for we hear nothing of great changes in the churches of the city. But steady changes there must have been, and in 1869 the 'new' practice of early morning Holy Communion was introduced into the Cathedral. The chief outward mark of the Church of England throughout the century was the rapid building of new churches, to keep pace with the growing population; thirty were built in Bristol between 1830 and 1870.

But the churches of the city had suffered a heavy blow in 1836. Parliament, in its reform of the Church of England, founded two much needed sees in Manchester and Ripon, to serve the great industrial areas of Lancashire and Yorkshire. But the money for them had to be found somewhere, and Bristol lost its bishopric. Perhaps it was in disgrace from the Bristol Riots. The Bristol diocese was amalgamated with Gloucester, its Dorsetshire section having been lopped off and given to Salisbury. The first Bishop of Gloucester and Bristol, James Henry Monk, saved the situation to a large extent by being really interested in his second Cathedral city. The Horfield Trust, for the upkeep of parsonages and the payment of curates, keeps alive the memory of his deep concern for all his flock. In 1877 the Cathedral at last received a nave, during the energetic Deanery of Gilbert Elliot. Elliot busied himself in persuading the authorities that Bristol deserved a see of its own. He succeeded in his efforts in 1883, when Gladstone supported the necessary Bill. He did not, however, live to see the carrying out of the proposal, which was delayed by financial difficulties until 1897. Bristol and Kingswood and the southern part of Gloucestershire, together with the northern part of Wiltshire, including Swindon, form the long-hoped-for Bristol diocese.

From the death of Queen Mary until the year 1791 it was illegal to hold Roman Catholic services in England. This does not mean, of course, that they were never held; many Roman Catholic families up and down the country maintained 'Recusant' priests in their household to say Mass for them and their fellow Roman Catholics. But it does mean that all this was done in great secrecy, and often with great danger. In the early part of the eighteenth century some brass-workers from the Rhineland and the Netherlands were invited to come to Bristol because of their extra skill. They refused to come unless they were allowed to go to Christian worship of their own choice—and they were Roman Catholics. So the Corporation, in the interests of Bristol's trade, closed its eyes to the law and allowed the Mass to be celebrated in a chapel at the foot of Ashley Hill. There were probably secret celebrations of the Mass in Bristol, as in other places, from time to time, and in 1790 a Roman Catholic Chapel and school were opened in Trenchard Street—just before the law was passed which allowed it to happen.

In 1828 came Catholic Emancipation; that is to say, Roman Catholics were at last allowed to enter Parliament and hold office in the State and in their own neighbourhood. Bristol did not welcome this measure very warmly, as we can see from the uproar which greeted Sydney Smith's sermon in favour of it on Guy Fawkes' Day, 1828. In 1843 St. Mary's on the Quay was opened as a Roman Catholic church, and in 1850 there was a Pro-Cathedral in Clifton and a Roman Catholic Bishop of Clifton. Several Roman Catholic schools and a Roman Catholic hospital (St. Mary's) have grown up in the city since then.

The Dissenters, like the Roman Catholics, were still prohibited from holding office at the beginning of the nineteenth century—until the year 1824, in fact—but in all other ways they played an important part in the life of the city. Many of the biggest and most famous firms were founded by them —J. S. Fry and Sons by a Quaker, W. D. and H. O. Wills by Congregationalists, E. S. and A. Robinson by a Baptist. They were building more and more chapels, too. A young man named John Hare came to Bristol to seek his fortune in the seventeen-sixties. He slept out on the night before he entered the city in an orchard in Bedminster. He had an encouraging dream, and when he awoke he vowed that if he prospered in business he would build a chapel on the spot where he had slept. He did prosper—considerably—by founding and building up a firm for the manufacture of oilcloth, which was painted afterwards to look like a Turkish carpet. So nearly sixty years after his arrival he gave the money for the building of Zion Chapel, Bedminster. It was opened in 1830, and in 1843 came the erection of Highbury Chapel, the first (but not the best) religious building designed by the famous architect, William Butterfield. It was put up on the spot where five Protestants are thought to have been put to death under Mary. The chapel had only two ministers during its first eighty years of life, David Thomas from 1844 to 1875, and his son Arnold from 1876 to 1924.

The Baptists moved their College for the training of ministers from Broadmead to Stokes Croft in 1811, and made a large increase in the number of their chapels during the century. One of the new ones, and later one of the most influential in the city, was Tyndale Church in Whiteladies Road. This was opened in 1869, and Richard Glover, the first minister of the church, was there for forty years. His only son was Terrot Reaveley Glover, who became Public Orator of Cambridge University and wrote many books about the Christian Faith, as well as about ancient Greece and Rome. His best-selling book was 'The Jesus of History', which gives an exciting account of the human life of Jesus. T. R. Glover always remained a staunch friend of Tyndale. When it was destroyed by enemy action during the Second World War, he at once sent a cheque for the re-building fund while most people were still gazing at the ruins.

It does not seem that the Quakers increased very much in numbers between 1800 and 1900. Except in their very early days it has not been their practice to try to gather in large numbers of converts. But they were as active as ever in furthering good causes. They took a leading part, for instance, in founding the Bristol General Hospital in 1832. The chief physician in the early days was John Addington Symonds, and his son of the same name was a well-known author who lived in Bristol for many years, and wrote some verses which are often sung as a hymn: 'These things shall be'.

The Unitarians gave Bristol one of the most forward-looking women of the century. Mary Carpenter was the eldest daughter of the minister of Lewin's Mead Chapel,

Lant Carpenter, who died in 1840. Before and after her father's death she carried out many schemes for helping poor people, and in 1845 a friend of hers, Lady Byron, widow of the poet, bought the Red Lodge in Park Row for her to use. Her idea was to have a school for girls who had been before the courts and to show them the possibilities of living a better kind of life than they were likely to embrace if they were sent to prison. She could not carry this out on a big scale, of course, but she pointed the way to an entirely new way of treating children who had broken the law, but needed education as much as punishment.

A much bigger enterprise was Müller's Orphanage. George Müller was a German, born in 1805. He lived a wild life as a youth, but in 1825 his whole way of living was changed, and he became a very earnest and zealous (though somewhat narrow) Christian. He emigrated to England, and worked in London for a Society which sought to convert Jews to Christianity. But bad health sent him to Teignmouth, where he joined the Plymouth Brethren. This group of Christians had recently been brought into existence by J. N. Darby, who believed that the whole of the Bible was dictated, word for word, by the Holy Spirit; he thought that the ordinary Churches had wandered a long way from the true faith, and he called on his followers to have nothing at all to do with worldly society or its pleasures; they were to meet each Sunday, without any ordained or paid minister, to 'break bread' as Jesus did at the Last Supper, and to hear the Word of God preached as it should be preached.

George Müller soon became a preacher and pastor among the Brethren, and moved to Bristol. Here the Brethren met with him in a Gospel Hall, now destroyed, in Great George Street. But he had great plans for looking after orphan children, and he began to carry them out in a house in Wilson Street, St. Paul's, in 1836. The Moravians had run Orphan Homes in Germany and America for a hundred and fifty years, and Müller wished to try the same methods in England. By our present-day standards the children were not allowed much freedom, and had to live in vast companies.

But in Müller's time, had it not been for Müller, very few orphans would have been looked after at all with any kindness whatever—and Müller, for all his strictness, loved children.

In 1849 he moved from Wilson Street to Ashley Down, and the great buildings (now taken over and increased for the College of Advanced Technology) were put up to house 2,000 children. Müller, of course, had no money of his own. He did not believe that Christians ought ever to ask for money, even for the best causes. So he simply prayed for the money he needed, and it always came, often just in time to pay the bills. At the age of seventy he set out to preach in four Continents, and died in Bristol in 1898 at the age of ninety-two. His work continues; nowadays, in accordance with modern ideas, it is carried on in smaller houses, where the children can belong to a family, in Backwell in Somerset and other places.

Of all the Christians who did not attend the parish churches it was the Methodists who increased most rapidly during the nineteenth century. But not in a united body. John Wesley had spent his greatest energies on bringing into the faith of Jesus Christ people who had little or no contact with the Churches, and many of the early Methodists were of this kind. But the later generations of Wesleyan Methodists (as those who kept strictly to the organisation of John Wesley were called) were not people who had been gathered into the Christian Church from an evil way of living. They were highly respectable people who had been Methodists all their lives. They quickly lost the art of appealing to the poor, ill-dressed, ill-mannered members of society. But other Methodists arose—often after breaking away from the Wesleyan Methodist Church—who were nearer to the spirit of John Wesley, although they had not the same devotion as he had to dignified worship and orderly Church government. One group was that of the Primitive Methodists, who had started in the Black Country under the leadership of Hugh Bourne and William Clowes in 1812, when they were not allowed to hold the kind of meetings they wanted to hold by the Conference of the Wesleyan Methodist Church. They wanted to hold 'Camp Meetings'—open-air gatherings which went on for a day or two, with many addresses and much public prayer. The Wesleyan Methodists were afraid that people would become too excited at such meetings, and also that they would be suspected of plotting against the Government (people were very nervous of this at this particular time). Bourne and Clowes went on with their Camp Meetings, and founded a separate Methodist Church which had a great appeal to the factory-workers, and helped them to form and run the early Trades Unions. They built several fairly small chapels in Bristol.

Then there were the Bible Christians. They began, not in any town, but in the Devonshire countryside at a place called Shebbear. William O'Bryan and James Thorne, their early leaders, had found the rules of the Wesleyan Methodists rather cramping, and preferred to launch out on their own. Their main strength was always in the West Country and the Isle of Wight, and they built several chapels in Bristol.

Meanwhile the Wesleyan Methodists were increasing steadily, and continued to do so until the biggest division of all took place in the middle of the century. This happened because a spirit of revolution was in the air, in church life as well as national life. A large number of Wesleyan Methodists, including many ministers, felt that they were being ordered about too much by a few men at the top, notably Jabez Bunting, who was the uncrowned king of the Methodists at the time. They began to publish pamphlets attacking the leadership, but did not put their names to them. Feelings ran very high, and in 1849 three well-known ministers were expelled by the Wesleyan Methodist Conference on the charge, which they would not deny, of having written the 'Fly Sheets' (the abusive pamphlets). The ministers took 100,000 members with them, and later formed the United Methodist Free Churches. This serious split in the ranks had its largest effects in Sheffield and other Northern towns, but Zion Methodist Church, Kingswood, and Hebron Methodist Church, Bedminster, are among several large chapels which were put up to give new places of worship to the rebels.

The Wesleyan Methodists recovered quickly from their disasters, and continued to increase until the end of the century. But they had learned the lessons of the conflict. They soon had a much more democratic method of ordering the affairs of their Church.

We have seen that the first schools for the poorer people were started at the beginning of the century by Christians who had seen that everyone has a right to education. In the latter part of the century three new Bristol schools which reached a high standard of education were started on Christian principles, though their fees have always tended to be beyond the reach of most people. John Percival was the virtual founder of Clifton College during his headmastership, which lasted from 1862 to 1879. He gave an equal status in the school to boarders and day boys, a most unusual thing in those days. He was also a moving spirit in the foundation in 1877 of Clifton High School for Girls, and helped to found Redland High School for Girls ten years later. One of his supporters in the foundation of Clifton High School was Catherine Winkworth, who translated several great German hymns into English, among them 'Now thank we all our God'.

It is clear from the last few pages that the second half of the century was a time of large congregations and many new churches. On Sunday, October 30th, 1881, the *Western Daily Press* arranged for all those who went to church to be counted. Two hundred and sixty-six thousand people altogether lived in Bristol then. On that day 48,596 people went to church in the morning and 60,856 in the evening (not including schoolchildren in either case); of these 109,452 churchgoers 45,518 were Anglicans, 15,363 Methodists (of all sorts), 11,588 Congregationalists, 10,146 members of the Salvation Army (which had just been started in London by William Booth, an ex-Methodist minister, for the poorest of the poor), 9,127 Baptists, 3,432 Roman Catholics; the rest belonged to small groups. So it seems that even at the height of churchgoing in this city many less than half the population went to church, though, of course, we cannot be quite sure of this.

The churches in Bristol would certainly not have been large enough to contain them all.

Yet the scene throughout the century was one of great and useful activity in all Church circles, so widely and deeply spread that there were few people, and fewer institutions, who were not helped, or at least affected, by it, whether they went to church or not. But apart from the failure to bring the Gospel to all the people in the city, there was one other great defect. Very few people seem to have been at all worried by the continued and increasing division of Christ's Church in the city into many, many separate Churches. Most people took the variety of denominations as a matter of course. Too many people still do.

CHAPTER 7

The Church Recalled To Unity

FOR THE FIRST FEW YEARS of the twentieth century, the period brought to a sudden and shocking end by the First World War of 1914 to 1918, things in Bristol and its churches went on much as before. The population was growing, trade and industry were healthy, the churches were full, life was fairly comfortable, except for the poor (and the reforms of Lloyd George in 1911 made things much better even for them by bringing in insurance against illness and unemployment), and most thinking people held the view that life was steadily getting better and better. Very few people foresaw the terrible crisis that was about to burst upon the world and change the whole direction of human life.

There was certainly progress in many parts of Bristol society. The chief sign of it was the Royal Charter given to Bristol University in 1909. There had been agitation for this for a long time. John Percival, the younger John Addington Symonds and Catherine Winkworth had all worked for it in Bristol; there was a Medical School, a Ladies' Association (for higher education, run by Miss Winkworth), and a Trade and Mining School (helped by the Merchant Venturers) by the early eighteen-seventies. Friends of Bristol in other places, notably Benjamin Jowett, Master of Balliol College, Oxford, were gaining support for the idea. It was first suggested that the Medical School should expand and become a University on its own. But Jowett and others insisted that the arts should be taught as well as the sciences, and,

after a famous meeting in the Victoria Rooms, University
College, for the teaching of science and literature, was opened
in 1876, with the Medical School and the Merchants' Technical School (once the Trade and Mining School) as sister

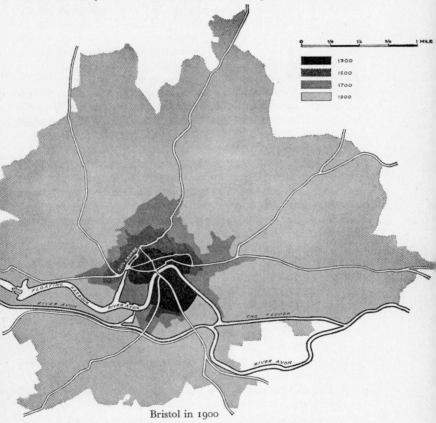

Bristol in 1900

Colleges. Women were admitted to University College from
the beginning.

So far, so good. But Bristol still wanted, and needed, a
University proper. The money was lacking, until at a dinner

in 1908, presided over by John Percival (by then a Bishop), it was announced that Mr. H. O. Wills would give £100,000 if a University could be created by uniting University College (of which the Medical School was by now a part) with the Merchants' Technical College. A petition was made to the Crown, and the Charter was granted. So, by the joint efforts of the Church, men and women of learning, and the business interests of the city, Bristol University was brought into being.

There were other, smaller signs of progress in these years. Western Academy, founded in 1752 to train Congregationalist ministers, had become Western College; after various homes it settled down in 1901 in Cotham, to be near University College and share its life as far as possible. With the same object in view the Baptist College, which had gained a great reputation in Baptist circles from the number of its past students sent out to the mission field in many parts of the world, moved in 1914 to a new building very near the University. These two Colleges were able to see to it that in the enthusiasm to pursue the new and fascinating subjects offered to its students by the University, the old study of the Bible and the Christian Faith was not forgotten.

Also in these years a greater degree of harmony was brought back to the Methodists by the union in 1907 of some of the smaller groups to form the United Methodist Church. In Bristol this chiefly meant the fusion of the Bible Christians and the United Methodist Free Churches. Thus for the next twenty-five years there were three Methodist Churches, the Wesleyan Methodist Church (the parent body), the Primitive Methodist Church and the United Methodist Church.

Very active in the life of the Baptist Churches in the early years of the century was a young man who was marked out to be one of the greatest Labour leaders and Foreign Secretaries that this country has produced. The mother of Ernest Bevin was a Somerset Methodist, but she died when he was seven, and he was brought up in Bristol as a Baptist. He was baptised, according to the custom of the Baptists, at the age of eighteen, and became a lay preacher. He went to the Bible Class of the Rev. Moffat Logan in Newfoundland Road, and was a member of St. Mark's Baptist Church, Easton, for many years. His Christianity soon began to find very practical expression in his efforts on behalf of the poor, and especially of the unemployed. He became a vigorous trade union organiser, and started a Committee called the 'Right to Work' Committee, to demand either work or maintenance for the unemployed. The City Council did not take much notice of this Committee—until Bevin carried out a dramatic gesture. He marshalled the unemployed one Sunday morning in the Horsefair, and marched them to the Cathedral. The authorities feared a riot; but Bevin led the men quietly into the Cathedral as the service started, and they sat there, starved, ragged and completely quiet. After the service they filed quietly out and dispersed. The Dean of Bristol led a deputation of leading Christians to the City Council to plead the cause of Bevin's Committee, and the Council agreed to make plans for the employment of the men.

The First World War did not destroy any buildings in Bristol. But it shattered innumerable lives, and hopes and dreams, and ways of thinking and ways of living. Like most cities in Europe, Bristol was robbed by the loss of those who did not come back from the War of a large proportion of those who should have maintained its life and health for the next few decades. Men and women in every Church and in every walk of life were called upon to re-think their whole attitude to life, religion and the society in which they lived. Sad to say, by no means every Christian, or every Christian Church, did the re-thinking that was needed. Many of the Churches, by trying to carry on as if nothing had happened, as if the world had not been turned upside down, completely failed to offer a home to the minds and spirits of those who did survive the War and of those who grew up in the post-War period. So the decline in churchgoing began which continued for a long time, and in some parts of the city is still continuing.

The War was followed by a few years of hope and apparent prosperity. Then came the dreadful slump of the later twenties, with unemployment, poverty and hardship in its

wake. Bristol, because of the variety of its trades and indus-
tries, had much less hardship to endure than the industrial
cities and towns of the Midlands and the North; but many
of its citizens suffered badly. Bristol recovered more quickly
than most in the nineteen-thirties, but in the shadow of a
war that could not be long delayed as Hitler rose to power
in Germany and beyond.

In 1924 some of the more wide-awake leaders of the British
Churches met in Birmingham for a 'Conference on Christian
Politics, Economics and Citizenship' (usually called 'Copec').
They issued statements on the Christian position in relation
to the great social problems of the time. Some of them were
Bristolians, and when they returned home they held a meeting in the Chapter House of the Cathedral to decide how to
carry further the unity which they had found in Birmingham.
They agreed to form the Bristol Council of Christian Churches,
one of the oldest, if not the oldest, of such Councils in this
country. All the Churches of the city were invited to join,
and the Council at once set on foot plans to deal with the
acute distress to be found in many places, not least by letting
houses and flats at low rents to families in need. In the
nineteen-thirties the Council's activities broadened out into
consultation between Bristol's Church leaders on all matters
of common concern to Christian people, and created a spirit
of harmony and goodwill between Christians of all denominations.

This kind of co-operation was a quite new thing, and a very
welcome contrast to the divisions and strife which had spoiled
the life of the Church in Bristol in the past. It was part of a
movement, known as the Ecumenical Movement (from the
Greek word 'oecumene', used of the 'inhabited world'),
which had begun at a great missionary conference in Edinburgh in 1910. Here nearly all the missionary societies
(except the Roman Catholic ones) had agreed on a joint
policy of advance in the Church overseas; and the idea of
planning Christian work and thought together (instead of
doing it in separate, watertight denominations) spread itself
into many parts of the Church in the whole world. One of

the consequences of the Edinburgh Conference was the formation of the Church of South India, out of the Anglican, Methodist, Presbyterian and Congregationalist Churches, in 1948; another is the foundation and activity of the World Council of Churches, to which all the great Churches of the world, except the Roman Catholic Church, belong. Bristol began to play its part in this great movement in 1925, and soon came to be thought of as one of its chief centres in Great Britain. C. S. Woodward and F. A. Cockin, past Bishops of Bristol, and now the present Bishop of Bristol, have given great support to the Bristol Council of Christian Churches, and the leaders of the other Churches have all done the same.

The period between the wars was in many ways a very grim one for those who could see what was really happening in this and other countries. But there were some bright features. One of them was the union of the three Methodist Churches into one Methodist Church in 1932, with far-reaching effects on the religious life of Great Britain. These were seen very clearly in Bristol, where Methodist churches of different kinds were very thick on the ground.

Another was the splendid benefaction of H. H. Wills and his wife in the foundation in 1925 of St. Monica's Home for elderly Anglican ladies too ill to run their own homes. Dame Monica Wills continued to give the Home her great care and attention after her husband's death until her own in 1931. The graceful buildings of the Home—and especially its chapel —on the Westbury edge of the Downs still provide peace and quiet even in the present noisy age.

The Second World War killed 1,229 people in Bristol by air-raid, and destroyed 3,000 houses, with a very large number of schools, churches and other public buildings; 90,000 houses and a correspondingly large total of other buildings were severely damaged. It also finally dislodged the last remnants of pre-1914 thinking and living. For a time, in 1940 and 1941, the full resources of Christians in the city, and indeed of all citizens, were directed to helping the bombed-out and injured, and maintaining at all costs the life of a city which was very important for the whole country, especially in view of aircraft manufacture at Filton. Later on in the War there was a little time for other things, though not for very much.

The Churches were certainly not inactive in providing homes and rest and clothes for the homeless, and comforts and companionship for men and women from the services quartered in the city or passing through it. As always in work which required the joint strenuous efforts of Christians of every Church, the Y.M.C.A. and Y.W.C.A. were to the fore. The Council of Churches found premises for the bombed-out, inside and outside the city; and in 1942 staged the first 'Religion and Life Week' of many to be held up and down the country during the latter part of the War. The object of the Week was to awaken Christians and others to the direct relation of the Christian Faith to family life, to education, to the spending of money and time, and to all problems of national and international life, and it is quite certain that the eyes of many previously blind Christians were opened by it.

In 1941 Mervyn Stockwood, Vicar of St. Matthew Moorfields (later Bishop of Southwark), called the ministers of the churches and chapels in Redfield to a service of Holy Communion in St. Matthew's. After the service they discussed with him what could be done by them all, working together, to bring the Gospel to the people of the neighbourhood, which was then ravaged by war. The Redfield ministers have met on every Tuesday morning since then for a similar purpose. The Redfield United Front was formed as a result of the first meeting; a united Youth Club was opened, and many kinds of united work, in the schools, in the open air, and in the factories have since been undertaken. More important still, the united work has been based on united worship, so that the Christians of Redfield have come to feel more and more that they belong to the one Church of Christ, rather than to a number of separate Churches. The Redfield United Front has provided a notable example for many similar movements in Bristol and far beyond.

The enterprises that have been begun in Bristol and its Church since the end of the War in 1945 must for many years be called experiments rather than achievements. But at least it can be said that the Churches were not caught napping by the War and its effects as they had been on a previous occasion. The existence of the Council of Churches and of the Redfield United Front, both admirably suited to deal with the problems of the post-war age, is sufficient evidence of this. And the planning for the future of the individual Churches fully bears out the statement.

The first job to be done was re-building, and this was taken in hand by all the Churches as soon as they could find the money from the War Damage Fund and their own resources. The next thing was to build new churches in the new housing estates which soon began to spring up on the outskirts of the city. There was no competition between the Churches in this matter. A joint committee of all the Churches organised the matter on the principle that in each new area there should be one parish church and one Free Church; the Free Churches, under the guidance of the Free Church Council, decided among themselves which should build a church in each new area as it appeared. The Bishop of Bristol raised a very large fund from business firms, large and small, as well as from individuals, and arranged for it to be divided out among all denominations. In the early days the shortage of materials made it impossible to allow more than a limited sum to be spent on any one church building, and all-purposes churches—churches, halls and Sunday School premises rolled into one—were put up in several places. When the restrictions were taken off it was possible to build churches more worthy of the best traditions of Bristol church-building in the past.

Long before the War many Churches had started youth clubs and other youth organisations, to cater for as many people under the age of twenty-one as possible. During the War everyone came to see how important it was that teen-agers should have clubs for useful activities of all sorts— games and dancing and more serious pursuits. After the

War was over, many youth clubs were started where there had been no such thing before, and all the Churches played a big part in this development.

The Church of England set out to do what it had never done so thoroughly before—arouse a deep interest in the Christian Faith among hosts of industrial workers who had never dreamed of going to church. The Bishop of Bristol appointed an Industrial Adviser who soon found his way into the largest factories in the city and just on the edge of it. A continuing series of conferences for boys and girls about to leave school for industry was also arranged.

The Methodist Church has made it a policy to take full advantage of Methodist Union in 1932 by rearranging its groups of churches ('circuits') in ways that will save man-power and expense, and by closing down churches no longer needed in order to release its resources in people and money for areas where churches are badly needed. It has brought Didsbury College for the training of ministers from its original home in Manchester, and so made up the number of such Colleges in Bristol to five—with the Baptist College, Western College, and the two Anglican Colleges, Clifton and Tyndale Hall. It has also set up an 'International House' in Clifton for students of all nations and creeds. Each of the larger Churches has a flourishing Society in the University.

There has been a large increase in joint activities by all the Churches, mostly under the auspices of the Council of Churches (now composed of more than a hundred and twenty congregations). In some ways the most important of these have been in small neighbourhood groups, where men and women have studied the Bible together, and to-gether considered the reasons why the Churches are still divided. They have not been able to end those divisions, but they have gone out to do many things together in the way of worship and house-to-house visitations and preaching the Gospel and supporting good causes.

The annual Week of Prayer for Christian Unity (started by the Roman Catholic Abbé Couturier, and devoted, not to the furtherance of any particular scheme for the union of

Churches, but to prayer that God will indicate the kind of unity that He wills) has been faithfully kept by a growing number of people, in a day of continuous prayer in the Cathedral, and in public meetings both in the centre of the city and in various neighbourhoods. The arrangement of religious broadcasts and television programmes in the West of England has helped to break down the barriers between the Churches, and all the activities of the Y.M.C.A., the Y.W.C.A., the Institute of Christian Education (for the assistance of teachers of the faith in schools), the British and Foreign Bible Society (which promotes the translation and distribution of the Bible all over the world), the Student Christian Movement, both in the University and in the sixth forms of schools, have furthered the same end. The Council of Churches has brought together the leaders of the Bristol Churches to discuss the great issues of the day (at the time of the Suez crisis in 1956 it issued a careful statement for the guidance of Christians, and held a great service of prayer in the Cathedral), and organised, usually in collaboration with the University, many series of lectures on the Bible, the unity of the Church and international affairs. Each Whitsun weekend it organises a conference at Shipham in Somerset, or elsewhere, for young people who are seriously concerned about the witness and unity of the Church.

The Churches of Bristol have learned, too, to look beyond their own affairs, not only to missions overseas (now much better called 'the life of the Church overseas'), but also to their nearer neighbours on the Continent of Europe. Soon after the War Bristol entered into alliances with Bordeaux and Hanover, cities of comparable size in France and Germany. Since then there has been a steady two-way flow of students, schoolchildren, civic leaders and officials, and many other groups, between the cities. For the Churches the alliance with Hanover has been easier to operate, since there is much community of religious opinion in this case. Bishop Hanns Lilje of Hanover, a notable and heroic opponent of Nazism during the War and after the War one of the really great leaders of the German Church, has been in Bristol several times; and his visits have been returned. On one occasion during the visit of Bristolians to Hanover one German after another rose in a meeting to thank the Christians of Bristol for their kindness and hospitality to German prisoners-of-war at the end of the War.

Then the Churches have made stupendous efforts to play a proper part in the solution of the world-wide refugee problem—efforts which culminated but did not end in World Refugee Year, 1959–60. They have constantly sought to keep the public conscience awake on this, as on many other vital issues of the twentieth century.

This is no mean output of united activity, and a great number of Christian thinkers believe that the Holy Spirit is working more in this than in any other way during the twentieth century. Yet this is not the view of all Christians and Christian congregations. Many stand aloof from it all—either because of deep religious convictions which prevent them from working with others, or because they are so busy with their own important affairs that they have no time or energy for the work that is being done by all Christians together. Moreover, Bristol has always been the home of many small religious bodies, with different degrees of resemblance in faith and practice to the larger Christian Churches. That has not ceased to be true. Since the War there has been a large increase of Pentecostalists, a group of people who believe every word of the Bible and hold that any Christian may receive the 'gift of tongues', the power to speak strange words at the command of the Holy Spirit. Some of these companies of intensely devout men and women have made more progress in numbers than the regular Churches.

Unity, nevertheless, has become more and more the key-note of Bristol Church life among those who look most keenly into the future. It seems clear that the problems which confront the Church can be solved much better by Christians praying and thinking together than by separate groups. Chief among such problems is that of putting the Christian Faith into words and sentences which the men and women of the twentieth century, most of them not brought up in Churches of any kind, can understand and accept. For this, and the whole task of the Church today, what is needed above all is a breed of Christians loyal to their own Churches, loyal still more to the one Church of Jesus Christ, and loyal above all to Jesus Christ Himself, the Head of the whole Church.

BIBLIOGRAPHY

Anglicanism, S. NEILL, Penguin.

The City and County of Bristol, B. LITTLE, Werner Laurie.

The Crisis of the Reformation, N. SYKES, G. Bles.

The English Free Churches, H. DAVIES, Home University Library.

A History of the Church in England, J. R. H. MOORMAN, A. & C. Black.

Hugh Latimer, H. S. DARBY, Epworth.

John Wesley, C. E. VULLIAMY, Epworth.

One Lord, One Church, J. R. NELSON, Lutterworth.

INDEX

Aidan, 4
Alban, 2
Almondsbury, 49, 77
Amsterdam, 39
Anabaptist, 21, 22
'Analogy of Religion', 58
Anglicans (see s. Church of England)
Anne, Queen, 53, 54
Ariminum, Council of, 2
Arles, Council of, 2
Asbury, Francis, 67
Assize Sermon, 79
Audland, John, 45, 46
Augustine, St., of Canterbury, 3, 4
Augustine, St., of Hippo, 2, 3, 8
Aust, 4, 14
Avignon, 13

Backwell, 84
Bacon, Robert, 43
Balliol College, Oxford, 13, 88
Baptists, 39, 40, 43–51, 56, 82, 86, 87
Barrow, Henry, 38
Bath, 1, 53, 70
Bell, Andrew, 77
Benedict, Rule of, 7
Benedict, St., 7
Berkeley de Gaunt, Maurice, 8
Berkeleys, the, 12
Bevin, Ernest, 90, 91
Bible Christians, 85, 90
Birmingham, 92
Blagdon, 76
Boleyn, Anne, Queen, 24, 26
Booth, William, 86
Bordeaux, 97
Bourne, Hugh, 84, 85
Bridewell, 48, 68
Bristol Baptist College, 23, 50, 57, 68, 82, 86, 90, 96
Bristol Council of Christian Churches, 92–97
Bristol Free Church Council, 95
Bristol General Hospital, 82
Bristol Grammar School, 33
Bristol Riots, 78
Bristol University, 88–90

British and Foreign Bible Society, 97
Browne, Robert, 38
Bunting, Jabez, 85
Burke, Edmund, 76
Bush, Bishop Paul, 29
Butler, Bishop Joseph, 58, 59, 64, 65
Butterfield, William, 82
Byron, Lady, 83

Caerlon, 2
Caerwent, 1
Callowhill, Hannah, 51
Calvin, John, 21, 36
Cambridge University, 23, 82
Camm, John, 45, 46
Camp Meetings, 85
Canynges, Joan, 14, 15
Canynges, John, 14, 15
Canynges, William, 14, 15
Carleton, Bishop Ralph, 49
Caroline, Queen, 58
Carpenter, Bishop John, 15, 16
Carpenter, Lant, 83
Carpenter, Mary, 82, 83
Carr, John, 34
Cathedral School, 33
Catherine of Aragon, Queen, 24
Cennick, John, 66, 67
Chapels and Churches:
  All Saints, City, 5, 57
  Assumption, Chapel of, 17
  Augustine's, St., Abbey, 8, 12, 28, 29, 41, 57, 78, 80, 91, 97
  Broadmead Chapel, 43–46, 49, 57, 82
  Castle Green Chapel, 45
  Cathedral (see s. St. Augustine's Abbey)
  Christ Church, City, 5
  Clifton pro-Cathedral, 81
  Ewin's, St., 5, 42
  George's, St., 58
  Hebron Methodist Church, Bedminster, 85
  Highbury Chapel, 31, 82
  Holy Trinity, City, 5
  James, St., Barton, 7, 65, 66
  John Street Chapel, New York, 67

INDEX

Chapels and Churches (*cont.*):
Lewin's Mead Chapel, 57
Lord Mayor's Chapel, 9, 31
Mark's, St. (*see s.* Lord Mayor's Chapel)
Mark's, St., Baptist Church, Easton, 90
Mary, Redcliffe, St., 12, 15, 50, 57
Mary-le-Port, St., 5
Mary, St., the Virgin, Oxford, 79
Mary's, St., on the Quay, 81
Matthew, St., Moorfield, 94
New Room, 65, 66, 72
Nicholas, St., 25
Old King Street Baptist Chapel, 44
Old King Street Methodist Chapel, 72
Paul's, St., 78
Peter's, St., 5
Philip's, St., 41
Portland Chapel, 67
Temple Church, 57
Thomas, St., City, 25
Trenchard Street Roman Catholic Chapel, 81
Tyndale Baptist Church, 82
Werburgh's, St., 5
Zion Chapel, Bedminster, 82
Zion Methodist Church, Kingswood, 85
Charles I, King, 40–44
Charles II, King, 44, 46–51
Cheddar, 76
Chi-Rho, 2
Church of England, 24 *et saepe*
Church of South India, 93
Churches (*see* Chapels and Churches)
Cirencester, 2
City School, 56
Clapham Sect, 76
Clarendon Code, 46
Clarkson, Thomas, 75
Clifton College, 86
Clifton High School, 86
Clifton Theological College, 96
Clowes, William, 84, 85
Cockin, Bishop F. A., 93
Coke, Thomas, 71
Colston, Edward, 56, 57
Colston's School, 57

Columba, St., 3
Congregationalists (*see s.* Independents)
Copec, 92
Cornwall, 30
Corporation Act, 51
Couturier, Abbé, 96
Coverdale, Miles, 28
Cowper, William, 75
Cranmer, Thomas, 24, 25, 30
Cromwell, Oliver, 44
Cromwell, Thomas, 24

Dagge, John, 68
Darby, J. N., 83
Didsbury College, 96
Dissenters, 46–52, 54–57, 71, 78, 79, 81
Dominic, St., 9, 10
Dominicans, 10, 25–27
Dunstan, St., 5

Ecumenical Movement, 92
Edinburgh, 92, 93
Edward the Confessor, King, 6
Edward II, King, 11
Edward IV, King, 15
Edward VI, King, 29–33
Elizabeth I, Queen, 31–39, 40, 41
Elizabeth Woodville, Queen, 15
Elliot, Gilbert, 80
Estlin, John Prior, 57
Evangelicals, 76, 77
Evans, Caleb, 57
Ewins, Mr., 45

Fell, Margaret, 46
'Fifteen Sermons', 58
Filton, 43, 94
Fitzharding, Robert, 8
'Fly Sheets', 85
Floke, John, 26
Fox, Edward Long, 58
Fox, George, 45, 46
Foy, Captain, 66
Francis, St., 9, 10
Franciscans, 10, 27
Fry, J. S., and Sons, 81

Gainsborough, 39
Gaunt, John of, 13
George II, King, 58

INDEX

INDEX